QUICK

◆

NAPKIN

◆

CREATIONS

———◆◆◆———

Making and Creating with Napkins

"In my hurried world, napkins provide a
refreshing oasis of texture, color, and shape.
What a fast, fun way to transform an
everyday meal into an extraordinary one!"

———— ◆◆◆ ————

*For my mother, Betty,
who makes napkins and buys everything else.*

ABOUT THE AUTHOR

With nine other sewing books and hundreds of articles to her credit, **Gail Brown** ranks as one of the most widely read sewing journalists, recognized for her innovative methods and writing style. Her work appears in *McCall's Pattern Magazine*, *Sew News*, *The Singer Sewing Library*, and *Vogue Patterns Magazine*, and she is a frequent guest on the "Sewing with Nancy" television show. She is also a Contributing Editor for the *Serger Update* and *Sewing Update* newsletters and has been an instructor for the Palmer/Pletsch Serger Workshops. Although this home-economics graduate started her career nearly 20 years ago in New York City, she now transmits via modem and facsimile from the small coastal town of Hoquiam, WA. Her patient husband, John Quigg, and two children, Bett and Jack, put up with her deadlines and growing collection of fabrics, sergers, sewing machines, needle-work collectibles, and Macintosh-computer paraphernalia.

Gail is currently working on a fast fabric-decorating book and after that, will finally finish a book (with Naomi Baker) on sewing and serging knits. (Both books will be offered by Open Chain.) Questions and comments from readers are welcomed. Write Gail c/o Open Chain Publishing,Inc., P.O. Box 2634-B, Menlo Park, CA 94026.

OTHER BOOKS BY THE AUTHOR:

Innovative Sewing: The Newest, Best, and Fastest Sewing Techniques (with Tammy Young)

Innovative Serging: The Newest, Best, and Fastest Overlock Techniques (with Tammy Young)

Creative Serging Illustrated (with Sue Green and Pati Palmer)

Creative Serging; The Complete Guide to Decorative Overlock Sewing (with Sue Green and Pati Palmer)

Sewing with Sergers (with Pati Palmer)

Sew a Beautiful Wedding (with Karen Dillon)

Sensational Silk

Super Sweater Idea Book (with Gail Hamilton)

QUICK NAPKIN
CREATIONS

MAKING AND CREATING WITH NAPKINS

GAIL BROWN

OPEN CHAIN PUBLISHING, INC.
Menlo Park, California

Acknowledgments

·····································

Published in Menlo Park, CA ,
by Open Chain Publishing, Inc.
PO Box 2634-B, Menlo Park, CA 94026.
(415) 366-4440
fax (415) 366-4455

ISBN 0-932086-23-3 softbound
ISBN 0-932086-24-1 hardbound

Library of Congress Catalog Card Number
90-063530

Color photographs by Lee Lindeman

Designed by Teddi Jensen

Illustrations by Bracey

Napkinmaking by Naomi Baker,
Gail Brown, and Virginia Fulcher

Some delightful props from Cate, Roy,
and Fran Keller

Printed in Hong Kong

♦ *Nearly every working day, I am sent
information and complimentary
samples from companies in the
home-sewing industry. Without this
generous ongoing support, I would
not be able to keep up-to-date with
the latest products or to develop new
techniques. To those many
companies who have helped me over
the last 20 years, thank you again.*

*My family and friends also
contribute daily to my writing
efforts. I am blessed with a husband
who accepts and encourages my
passion for sewing journalism (even
when I must work in the evenings
and on weekends). I am spurred on
by my two children, Bett and Jack,
who ask, "How many pages did you
finish today, Mom?" My dear friend
and fellow free-lancer, Naomi Baker,
spends countless hours sharing her
unparalleled sewing knowledge.
Our very busy household, which
also doubles as my office, is
prevented from slipping into total
chaos by Donna Cook; I simply
couldn't work without her help.*

*Acknowledgment is also well
deserved by those who made my
words come to life in this book—
my artist, Bracey; my designer,
Teddi Jensen; my photographer, Lee
Lindeman; and my sample
napkinmaker, Virginia Fulcher.
Robbie Fanning makes it all happen,
wearing a multitude of hats—as
editor, accountant, photo stylist,
print buyer, salesperson, napkin-
technique tester, and friend.*

Why I Love Napkinmaking (And Why You Might Too)

❖ *I can make napkins quickly, with or without a sewing machine or serger.* In fact, I can complete a six-napkin set in 20 minutes (or less).

❖ *The napkins I make look better, last longer, and are more affordable than comparable ready-mades.* Plus, I don't have to settle for second-best when it comes to the color, fabric, or quantity.

❖ *There's not a more welcomed gift.* In far less time and with far less money than required for gift shopping, I make napkin sets for showers, weddings, birthdays, and housewarmings.

❖ *When making napkins, I don't have to worry about fitting*, as I do when making clothes, slipcovers, or curtains.

❖ *Folding napkins makes tablesetting fun.* My daughter actually volunteers to set the table when napkin folding is part of the task.

❖ *Napkins transform an everyday meals into a dining "event."* There's simply something special about a table set with napkins.

❖ When sewing any square and rectangle (scarves and tablecloths, for instance), *I borrow from my napkinmaking expertise to finish edges and corners fast and professionally.*

❖ *I can find inexpensive napkinmaking materials everywhere*—in thrift shops, linen closets and departments, fabric stores (especially discounted remnants and flat folds), upholstery shops (sample cuts are favorites), and of course, my fast-multiplying fabric stash.

❖ With a little ingenuity, *my finished napkins can become gift wraps, decorative lampshade covers, basket liners, placemats, valances, or chair tidies.*

So when Robbie Fanning asked me to write about napkinmaking, I jumped at the opportunity. A new approach to book-writing was another underlying incentive: I've always thought that sewing and fabric-crafting books should be more like cookbooks, and more fun. So we set up this book like a cookbook. Need to whip up a napkin? Follow an easy "recipe" on any of the project pages of this book—each technique is inclusive, taking you through the entire process in one or two pages.

Enjoy making, folding, and creating with your napkins.

GAIL BROWN

P.S. Please stay in touch. Send your questions, comments, and yes, even criticisms to me c/o **Open Chain Publishing, Inc.** P.O. Box 2634-B, Menlo Park, CA 94026. (415) 366-4440

C O N T

E   N   T   S

Quickest Napkinmaking,
Step-by-Step

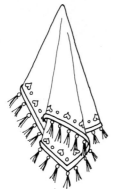

1. **Peruse the book.** There are 18 techniques, each one numbered and photographed in a different fold. The techniques are divided into three distinct categories: *No-Sew, Easy-Sew,* and *Serged.* If you don't have time to make a napkin, skip to Step 6.

2. **Match your talents, time, and equipment to the techniques described in this book.** The "Fastest, Faster, Fast Napkinmaking" chart on page 9 should help you decide. (Note that all techniques are some degree of fast.) Also, each chapter is organized in order of technique ease, with the easiest in the category first.

3. **Gather your napkinmaking tools, fabrics, and notions.** "The Materials" required are listed on each project page. Also see the fabric-selection, marking, cutting, and notion tips in "The Napkinmakers' Time-and Money-Saving Guide," page 73.

4. **Maximize the number and size of your napkins,** by consulting the yardage charts on pages 86 – 91. For example, you can cut nine 15" (38cm) (unfinished) napkins from a 1-1/4 yard (1.1 meters) of 45" (115cm)-width fabric, without wasting an inch.

5. **Whistle while you work.** Napkinmaking is fun. Don't fret about boo-boo's— I guarantee you, no one will notice.

6. **Have fun folding napkins.** Step-by-step how-to's are given for all the folds shown in photography. (See the "Featured Napkin Folds: Fast, Fun, and Press-free," pages 10 – 16.) You'll find the folds are, indeed, fast, fun and press-free.

7. **Utilize napkins for innovative non-table purposes,** such as the gift wrap, decorative accessories, and pillows shown in Chapter IV, "Napkins Do Double-Duty," page 67.

8. **Revel in all the compliments.** Watch out—your family and friends will request several additional napkin sets. Get ready to make more—return to Step 2.

Fastest, Faster, Fast Napkinmaking

Fastest	Technique (Requirements)
1. PINK NOW, SEW (MAYBE) LATER (PAGE 20)	Pinked technique (sharp pinking shears required)
WHY DIDN'T-I-THINK-OF-THAT? NAPKINS (PAGE 30)	Instant napkins (no gluing, cutting, sewing, or serging required)
6. LINED NAPKINS— IN MINUTES! (PAGE 34)	Sewn technique (basic straight-stitch machine required)
7. TWIN-NEEDLE TOP-STITCHED (page 36)	Twin-needle technique (zigzag machine that threads from front to back and twin needle required)
15. SERGED, TURNED, & TOP-STITCHED (PAGE 58)	Serged technique (2- or 3-thread serger and two or three spools or cones of thread required)
16. NARROW ROLLED-EDGE FINISH (PAGE 60)	Serged technique (2- or 3-thread serger with rolled-edge capability and two or three spools or cones of thread required)
17. UNROLLED-EDGE FINISH (PAGE 62)	Serged technique (2-or 3-thread serger with two or three spools or cones of thread required)

Faster	
2. FRINGE NOW SEW LATER (PAGE 22)	Fringed technique (loosely woven fabric and basic sewing machine required)
3. FABRIC-FRINGED EDGES (PAGE 24)	Fabric-fringed technique (sharp shears or scissors and tightly woven fabric required)
5. FAST-FUSED EDGES (PAGE 28)	Fused technique (fusible-transfer web and steam iron required)
9. NARROW HEM, POSTHASTE (PAGE 40)	Serged and sewn technique (both a 2- or 3-thread serger and a basic sewing machine required)
12. EASY TRIMMED EDGES (PAGE 46)	Sewn and trimmed technique (basic straight-stitch machine and washable trim required)
13. HIDDEN-SEAM TRIM FINISH (PAGE 48)	Sewn and trimmed technique (basic straight-stitch machine and washable trim required)
14. NO-MEASURE MITERS (PAGE 50)	Sewn technique (basic straight-stitch machine required)
18. LAPPED-TRIM FINISH (PAGE 64)	Serged and sewn technique (both a 2- or 3-thread serger and a basic sewing machine and washable trim required)

Fast	
4. GREAT GLUE! TRIMMED HEMS (PAGE 26)	Glued and trimmed technique (washable glue and trim required)
8. HEMMED AND SATIN-STITCHED EDGES (PAGE 38)	Sewn technique (basic zigzag machine required)
10. DOUBLE SATIN–STITCHED EDGES (PAGE 42)	Sewn technique (basic zigzag machine required)
11. DECORATIVELY MACHINE-STITCHED EDGES (PAGE 44)	Decoratively machine-stitched (sewing machine with decorative-stitch capability required)

FEATURED NAPKIN FOLDS: FAST, FUN, AND PRESS-FREE

FEATURED FOLDS:

1. Round-Up Tie
2. Valentine
3. Beginner's Delight
4. Into the Sunset
5. Easy Folds
6. Twin Peaks
7. Flaming Flower
8. Simple Elegance
9. Instant Drape
10. Flying Ascot
11. Spiraled Fold-Up
12. Easy Roll-Up, Tied or Ringed
13. Napkin Nosegay
14. Double-Point Pocket
15. Soft Folds in a Ring
16. Soft, Quick Candlestick
17. Spiral
18. Napkin Knot-in-no-Time

Even if you never make a napkin, you shouldn't miss the fun of folding. Every photograph in this book features a fast-folding technique; all folds can be finished in thirty seconds (or less), and don't require pressing or extra-large napkin sizes.

FAST-FOLDING TIPS

◆ *Fold on the table or any clean, flat surface* (much easier and more accurate than attempting to fold "in the air").

◆ *Select a fold that will show off napkin embellishments.* For instance, "10. Flying Ascot" would showcase an appliquéd or monogrammed corner beautifully.

◆ *If the fold stands on a plate or in a glass, use a crisp napkin.*

◆ *To enhance crispness, use press-on starch.* Follow the label instructions and cautions.

◆ *If using a soft napkin fabric, stick with draped or tied folds,* such as "3. Beginner's Delight," "9. Instant Drape," "15. Soft Folds in a Ring," or "18. Napkin Knot-in-no-Time."

◆ *Beef up a limp napkin by folding it with a contrasting- or blending-color napkin,* wrong sides together.

◆ For more a more dramatic fold (and table setting), *experiment with larger-than-usual (20"+) napkin sizes.* (When you make your own, you're not restricted to smallish ready-mades.)

◆ *Try rolling up rectangular napkins.* See the "8. Simple Elegance" and "12. Easy Roll-Up, Tied or Ringed."

◆ *To accessorize your table, secure folds, and maximize the napkin size, use rings.* See "Instant and Semi-Instant Napkin Rings," page 80.

◆ *Store your napkins unfolded,* so they'll be ready for the next folding session.

◆ *Don't let stodgy table-setting rules put a crimp in your creativity.* Follow my only rule: use napkins whenever and wherever you like.

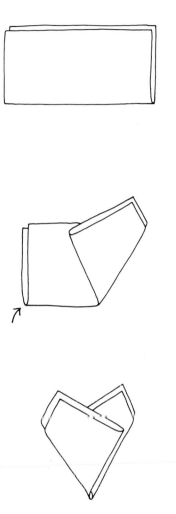

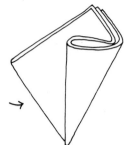

1.

ROUND-UP TIE

2.

VALENTINE

3.

BEGINNER'S DELIGHT

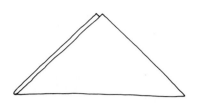

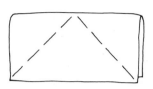

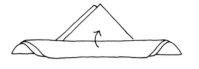

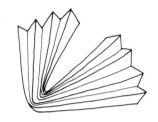

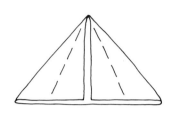

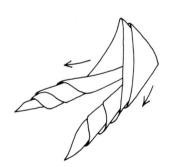

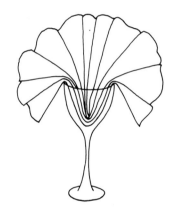

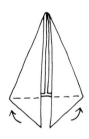

4.

INTO THE SUNSET

5.

EASY FOLDS

6.

TWIN PEAKS

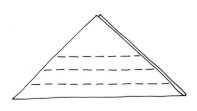

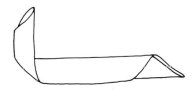

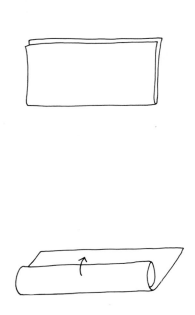

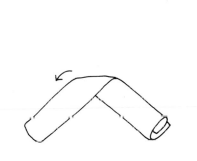

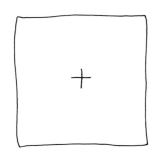

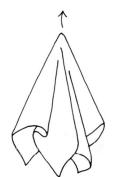

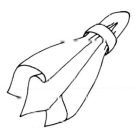

7.

FLAMING FLOWER

8.

SIMPLE ELEGANCE

9.

INSTANT DRAPE

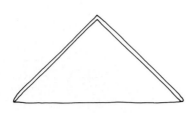

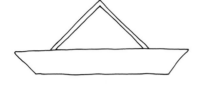

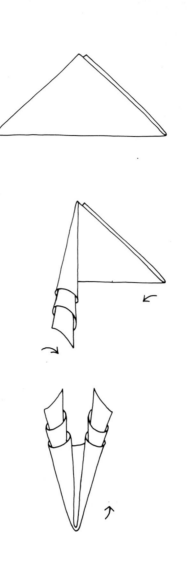

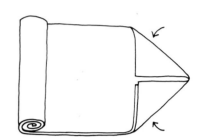

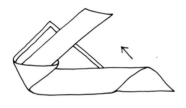

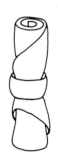

10.

FLYING ASCOT

11.

SPIRALED FOLD-UP

12.

**EASY ROLL-UP,
TIED OR RINGED**

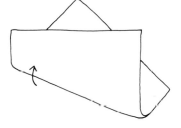

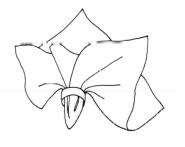

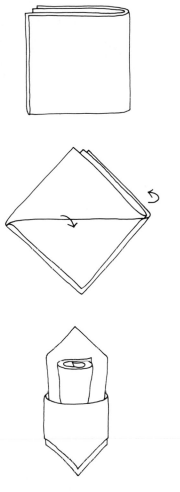

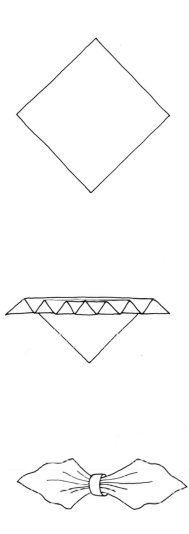

13.

NAPKIN NOSEGAY

14.

DOUBLE-POINT POCKET

15.

SOFT FOLDS IN A RING

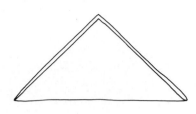

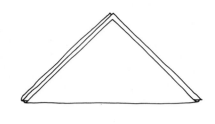

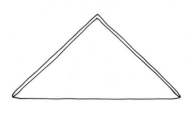

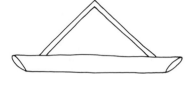

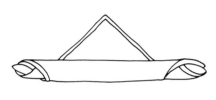

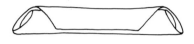

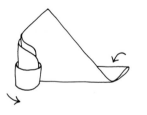

16.

SOFT, QUICK CANDLESTICK

17.

SPIRAL

18.

NAPKIN KNOT-IN-NO-TIME

So You Don't Have the Time or Inclination to Sew: No-Sew Napkin Options

Goof-Proof Gluing Primer

❖ *Prewash the fabric and trims before gluing.* Washing will remove finishes that can prevent the glue from absorbing into the fabric.

❖ *To save your table tops, work on a disposable or reusable "gluing board."* I reserve one side of my June Tailor *Craft 'n Needlework Board* for gluing, but any large piece of cardboard, such as the cheap fold-up cutting boards, do the job.

❖ *Use permanent washable glue* for glued methods. *Do not use white craft glue for napkin-making; it will wash out.* There are two types of washable glues: *solvent (acetone)-based* (the clear, stinky kind), which are both washable and usually (but not always) dry-cleanable; and *waterproof* (usually off-white and gloppy), which can be washed but generally not dry-cleaned. Solvent-based permanent glues include Beacon Chemical Company's *Fabri Tak*, Bond's *527™*, *EZ Fabric Glue*, Magic American Chemical's *Fabric Mender™ Magic*, and Washington Millinery's *Bridal Glue*. Waterproof glues include Aleene's *OK-to-Wash-It™*, Jurgen's *Jewel & Fabric Glue,* Plaid's *Glu-N-Wash*, or W.H. Collin's *Unique Stitch™*. One 1-1/4-ounce (or larger) tube or bottle should be sufficient for a set of six napkins, but if you like gluing and hate repeated trips to the store, buy the biggest container available.

❖ *Choose the right glue for your fabric and trim.* Solvent-based glues bleed less through synthetic or synthetic-blend fabrics, trims, and embellishments, but dry stiffer than waterproof glues. For natural-fiber fabrics, waterproof glues work well and dry a little more flexibly than solvent-based glues. For maximum durability, a solvent-based glue might anchor the napkin corners, while a more flexible waterproof glue might hem the sides. No matter what glue you use, the bond will be more durable and softer on natural-fiber fabrics or blends composed of 20% or less synthetic fiber.

If you notice the glue bleeding through to the right side of the napkin, it probably means that your fabric is too lightweight for this method, or that you should switch to a solvent-based glue. (All-over prints and checks camouflage bleed-through much better than solid colors.)

❖ *If using solvent-based glues, follow safety precautions.* Glue in a well-ventilated room, away from any sparks, fire, or flame. Grade-school-age kids should be supervised while gluing.

❖ After applying the glue, *allow it to become tacky, before attempting to glue fabric or fabric/trim layers together.*

❖ *Finger- and book-press when gluing.* Finger-press glued edges together to glue-baste a hem or trim in place (Fig. I-1). After you've glued all the edges, use the weight of a couple large books to press then napkin as it dries. See Fig. I-1 on page 19.

❖ *For flattening glued corners, try tapping with a rubber mallet* (sold at leather-crafting stores such as Tandy's). If you don't have a rubber mallet around (most people don't), just cover the end of a hammer with a couple of wash rags.

❖ *Clean off excess glue residue* by simply rubbing it off (use clean fingers, please). Waterproof glues can be removed with special products like Plaid's *Glu-N-Wash NO-SPOT Adhesive Solvent.* Acetone (use the milder form, fingernail polish remover) will dissolve solvent-based glues, but may also remove some fabric color.

❖ *Allow ample drying time for glues.* I let mine dry overnight before using the napkins, and particularly before laundering.

❖ *To soften the edges, steam-press glued napkins after machine drying.* Then, after they've cooled, store the napkins flat rather than folded. (Glued edges tend to mold to the shape of the fold.)

❖ *Simply reglue any part of the hem that comes loose during laundering.*

No-Hassle, No-Sew Tips

❖ *Test any prospective edge-finishing method on scraps of your napkin fabric.* (You will no doubt get sick of this reminder.) Doing so will not only help you perfect the technique, but will help determine the suitability of your fabric. Not happy with the results, but like the technique? Try another fabric. Conversely, if you like the fabric but not the results, try a different technique.

❖ *Remember that glued and fused edges will be stiffer than sewn or serged edges.* Compensate by using light- to medium-weight, flat, tightly constructed fabrics. Refer to "Fabric Possibilities," page 76.

❖ *Use fusible transfer web*, the paper-backed kind, such as Aleene's *Hot Stitch Fusible Web,* HTC's *Trans-Web™,* J & R's *Magic Fuse™* (now distributed by Dritz), Pellon's *Wonder-Under™,* Speed Stitch's *Fusible Film™,* or Thermo Web's *Heat N Bond* (see "Mail-Order Sources," page 94). The new precut 3/4" (2cm)-wide fusible transfer web tapes, sold on rolls by both HTC (*Trans-Web Tape™*) and Pellon (*Wonder-Under™ Transfer Fusing Web* tape), are handy for the "5. Fast-Fused Edges," page 29.

Whatever fusible you choose, follow the package or interleaf instructions, steam-pressing the full ten-second count in each area. (Brands differ, web to web. Test to compare ease of use, bulk, adherence, and price.)

Also, be on the lookout for the new liquid fusibles, such as Beacon Chemical Company's *Liquid Thread™* and Bond's *Fabric Glue #430;* when pressed between two fabrics, these nontoxic glues create permanent bonds similar to fusible-transfer web.

❖ *Banish bulk by trimming corners* as described for each napkin technique.

Fig. I-1. *Finger-press glued hems.*

PINK NOW, SEW (MAYBE) LATER

◆ 1 ◆

No, it's not a bandanna scarf,
but a Western-inspired napkin
fold, perfect when nestled on
any plate. And yes, the edges
are finished in a flash with
pinking.

NO-SEW ◆ TECHNIQUE

The Materials

❖ *Fabrics and linings shown here*: 100% cotton contrasting-color bandanna prints, fused together at the edges (see *Variations,* below). Refer to "Fabric Credits," page 95. Or any tightly woven fabric (those with a glazed finish, such as chintz, are especially ravel-resistant). *Do not prewash the fabric; fabric finishes facilitate cleaner cutting.*

❖ *Sharp pinking or scalloping shears*

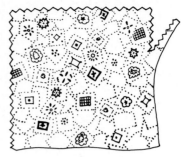

Fig. 1-1. *Pink or scallop to finish edges.*

The Steps

1. Using regular sewing shears, cut out the napkin squares allowing 1/2" (1.3cm) on all sides.

2. Using the pinking or scalloping shears, carefully pink or scallop to finish the edges, trimming off about 1/2" (1.3cm). See Fig. 1-1.

CUTTING TIP:

Don't manhandle those shears. You'll cut a cleaner, more even edge, if you take short half-blade strokes and let the blades fall together effortlessly. See Fig.1-2.

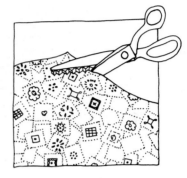

Fig. 1-2. *For cleaner cutting, take easy, half-blade strokes.*

VARIATIONS:

Topstitch or fuse napkin and lining layers together, then pink the edges. See Fig. 1-3 and the napkins shown in the photograph, left.

TO SEW OR NOT TO SEW, LATER:

When we tested laundering a tightly woven cotton chintz that had been pinked, the edges didn't ravel at all. But if you do opt for finishing before laundering, simply turn up the pinked hems 3/8" (1cm) to the wrong side and top-stitch 1/4" (6mm) from the edge fold (Fig. 1-4).

Or stick with no-sewing: permanently glue the pinked hems 3/8" (1cm) to the wrong side (Fig. 1-4).

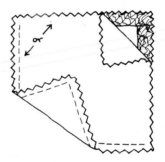

Fig. 1-3. *Variations: Topstitch or fuse napkin and lining together, then pink or scallop the edges.*

The Fold

See the step-by-step folding how-to's for *1. Round-Up Tie* on page 11.

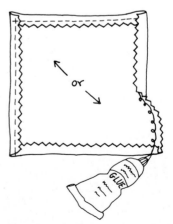

Fig. 1-4. *Optional: Hem and stitch or glue.*

FRINGE NOW, SEW LATER

◆◆ *2* ◆◆

*Fringing is fast and can be
done while watching TV or
commuting. I recruit others to
help: my husband would
rather fringe than move the
furniture.*

NO-SEW ◆ TECHNIQUE

The Materials

❖ *Fabrics shown here:* 100% cotton two-tone homespun and 50% polyester/50% polyester linen-like. Refer to "Fabric Credits," page 95. Or any other loosely woven fabric. Remember, the easier the fabric is to fringe, the greater the necessity for sewing before laundering.

❖ *Large hand needle* to help pick out the fabric threads.

The Steps

1. Neatly cut out the napkin squares using sharp shears.

2. Mark the fringe depth with transparent tape, as shown. Fringe the napkin, crosswise sides first, to a depth of about 1" (2.5cm). See Fig. 2-1. Use the needle to dislodge stubborn threads.

CUTTING TIP:

Instead of cutting separate napkins, cut napkin strips along the crosswise grain of the fabric. Fringe the entire width of the fabric, then fringe along the lengthwise grain to form the napkin squares. See Fig. 2-2.

DO SEW LATER, BEFORE LAUNDERING:

When I tested laundering one of these loosely woven, fringed napkins, the base of the fringe started unraveling. Stitching before laundering is highly recommended: straight stitch, narrow zigzag, or decoratively machine stitch along the base of the fringe, using a medium-length stitch (Fig. 2-3). If you have time to sew before fringing, your stitching line can be the depth guideline for the fringing.

The Fold

See the step-by-step folding how-to's for **2. Valentine** on page 11.

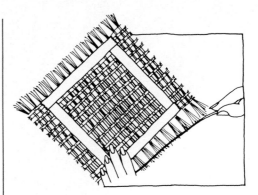

Fig. 2-1. *Fringe opposite sides first, to tape markings.*

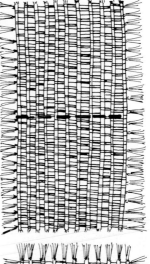

Fig. 2-2. *Fringe crosswise-grain edges first, then along lengthwise-grain edges*

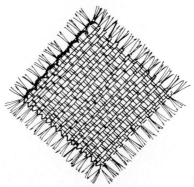

Fig. 2-3. *Optional but recommended: before laundering, straight stitch, zigzag, or decoratively stitch along base of fringe.*

Fabric-Fringed Edges

— ◆◆ 3 ◆◆ —

*A Southwestern-look scarf
with beaded self-fabric fringe
inspired me: without the
beads, wouldn't the cut-fringe
be a perfect no-sew napkin
edge finish?*

NO-SEW ◆ TECHNIQUE

The Materials

❖ **Fabrics and linings shown here:** 100% cotton contrasting-color Southwestern-inspired prints. Refer to "Fabric Credits," page 95. Or, for both the napkin and lining, any light- to medium-weight tightly woven fabric such as broadcloth, chambray, calico, or decorator prints.

❖ **Fusible transfer web (paper-backed, see page 19):** 1/4 yard (.2meters) of 18" (46cm)-wide web for each 18" (46cm) napkin.

❖ **Transparent tape (the cloudy kind), such as Scotch Magic™ Tape.**

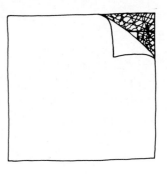

Fig. 3-1. *Fuse edges of napkin and lining together.*

The Steps

1. Carefully cut out the napkin and lining squares. Using 2" (5cm)-wide strips of fusible transfer web, fuse together the wrong sides of the napkin and lining (Fig. 3-1).

2. Place tape 2" (5cm) from all the edges. See Fig. 3-2.

3. Using sharp scissors, cut 1/2" (1.3cm)-wide, 2" (5cm)-deep fringe (to the tape), angled at 45 degrees to minimize ravelling, along all edges. "Eyeball" the strip width, checking the measurement intermittently. Change the fringe-angle direction as shown. See Fig. 3-2.

4. Remove the tape. Use napkin as is, or wash first, to enhance the raggy look. (Loose threads can be quickly trimmed.)

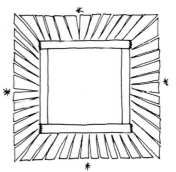

Fig. 3-2. *Cut fringe to tape, changing angle direction at * markings.*

OPTIONAL:
For increased durability, or thread-color contrast, zigzag or straight stitch (with a single or twin needle) along the base of the fringe (Fig. 3-3).

VARIATION:
These napkins can also be made single layer, although the fringed edges will ravel more without the stabilization of a fusible web. Use a tightly woven medium-weight fabric such as denim or chino.

The Fold

See the step-by-step folding how-to's for *3. Beginner's Delight* on page 11.

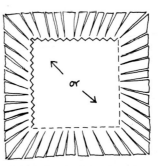

Fig. 3-3. *Optional: Zigzag or straight stitch along base of fringe.*

GREAT GLUE! TRIMMED HEM

◆◆ 4 ◆◆

*Gluing trim or ribbon to the
napkin-hem edges effectively
decreases bulk, puckering, and
production time, while adding
a snappy accent. Great fun!*

NO-SEW ◆ TECHNIQUE

The Materials

❖ **Fabrics shown here:** 100% cotton yarn-dyed plaid and 100% cotton linen-like polka-dot print. Refer to "Fabric Credits," page 95. Or any *prewashed* moderately to tightly woven, light- to medium-weight fabric with no discernible right or wrong side.

❖ **Permanent washable glue** (refer to brands on page 18).

❖ **Trims shown here:** 100% polyester 3/8" (1cm)-wide polka-dot grosgrain and 100% polyester 1" (2.5cm)-wide ribbon. Or any 3/8" – 3/4" (1 – 2cm)-wide, *prewashed* trim or ribbon, such as satin or grosgrain, that the glue won't bleed through. You'll need the finished perimeter plus 4" (10cm), or about 1-2/3 yards (1.5 meters) for each 14" (36cm) finished napkin or about 2 yards (1.8 meters) for each 17" (43cm) finished napkin.

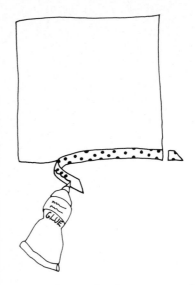

Fig. 4-1. *Apply glue to trim and lap over edge.*

The Steps

1. Cut out napkin squares, allowing 1/2" – 1" (1.3 – 2.5cm) hems on all sides.

2. Cut the trim into four equal lengths for each napkin. Apply glue to the wrong side of one trim length. Working on a gluing board (see page 18), lap the glued trim half its width over the the wrong side of one raw edge (Fig. 4-1); cut off any excess trim.

3. Apply glue to the right side of the hem edge, 1/2" – 1" (1.3cm – 2.5cm) from the edge. Finger press a 1/2" – 1" (1.3 – 2.5cm)-wide hem; trim the corner to minimize bulk. See Fig. 4-2. Repeat for the opposite side.

4. Repeat Steps 2 and 3 for the other pair of opposite sides, folding miters at the corners as shown in Fig. 4-3. (Dab glue on the wrong side of the corner fold for a more secure bond.)

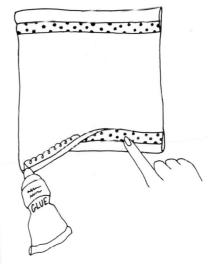

Fig. 4-2. *Glue hem and finger-press.*

The Fold

See the step-by-step folding how-to's for *4. Into the Sunset* on page 12.

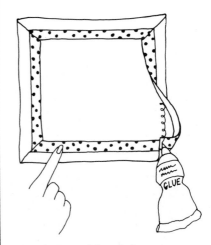

Fig. 4-3. *Fold and glue miter.*

FAST-FUSED EDGES

—◆◆ 5 ◆◆—

*If you'd rather press than sew,
this technique's for you. Fusing
eliminates raveling and is a
nifty alternative when your
machine isn't with you.*

NO-SEW ◆ TECHNIQUE

The Materials

- ❖ *Fabrics shown here*: 100% cotton holiday prints. Refer to "Fabric Credits," page 95. Or any light- to medium-weight *tightly woven* fabric.

- ❖ *Fusible transfer web* (paper-backed) strips—one 15-yard roll (13.7meters) (see page 19) of 3/4" (2cm)-width is enough for about seven 18" (46cm)-square napkins. Or cut your own—buy 1/8 yard (4-1/2" or 11cm) of 18" (46cm)-wide web for each 18" (46cm) square (or smaller) napkin. (For "Mail-Order Sources," see page 94.)

The Steps

1. Carefully cut out the napkin squares. (The raw edges will be exposed.)

2. Fuse 3/4" (2cm)-wide strips of fusible-transfer web to the wrong side of two opposite edges, as shown (Fig. 5-1).

   ### JELLY-ROLL CUTTING TIP:
   If you cut your own web strips, ensure uniformly even strips by rolling the transfer web in the crosswise direction and cutting into 3/4" (2cm)-wide rolls (Fig. 5-2).

3. Remove the transfer-web paper. Carefully finger-press a 3/8" (1cm) hem along the sides shown (Fig. 5-3), completely covering the web; the two webbed edges will adhere instantly. Press.

4. Repeat Steps 2 and 3 for the opposite sides (Fig. 5-4). Any threads loosened by laundering can be easily clipped to neaten the exposed edges.

The Fold

See the step-by-step folding how-to's for *5. Easy Folds* on page 12.

Fig. 5-1. *On wrong side, fuse 3/4" (2cm)-wide transfer-web strips to opposite edges.*

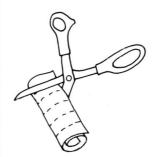

Fig. 5-2. *Jelly-roll cutting tip: Roll web, then cut every 3/4" (2cm).*

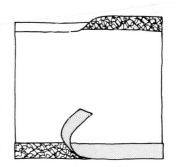

Fig. 5-3. *Remove web paper and finger-press 3/8" (1cm)-wide hems.*

Fig. 5-4. *Repeat fusing and finger-pressing (Steps 2 and 3) for remaining opposite sides.*

Why-Didn't-I-Think-of-That? Napkins

Each time I discover another instant, non-traditional napkin, my thought is,"Why didn't I think of that?" The terrycloth hand towel, for instance, makes terrific sense: if you're going to get messy eating clams or spaghetti, why not spiff up with a super-absorbent napkin fabric? And for Woolworth's price of $1.00, you can buy dozens of bandannas to use as napkins for picnic and barbecues, plus a few extra to wear as head scarves.

❖ *Be creative.* Use 15" (38cm) square, or if rectangular, 15" (38cm) along one side or larger cotton bandannas; cotton, rayon, or acrylic (or any washable) scarves or hankies; linen, ramie, or cotton hand towels; or terrycloth hand towels or large washcloths. My editor, Robbie Fanning, has even used diapers (no kidding—don't worry, they were bought new at a craft fair). For large quantities of napkins, consider mail-order catalog sales; you can buy quantities larger than generally available at retail stores, sometimes at discounted prices.

Fig. I-2. *Bandannas as napkins*

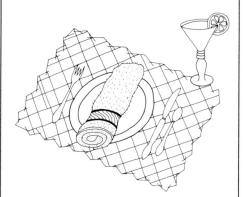

Fig. I-3. *Terrycloth hand towels as napkins*

❖ *Look for unusual prints, intense colors, and distinctive textures* that help these wardrobe, kitchen, and bathroom accessories fake it as napkins.

❖ *Enhance or improve less-than-desirable or un-napkin-like edges* by adding machine stitching, serging, or trims. Refer to "For Napkins Made or Ready-Made: No-Sew Embellishments," pages 54 and 66 and "Doctoring Dull (And Otherwise Undesirable) Ready-Mades," page 79.

Fig. I-4. *Cotton scarves as napkins*

Fig. I-5. *Kitchen hand towels as napkins*

MISTAKE-PROOF
MACHINE-SEWN NAPKINS

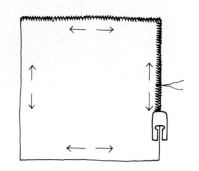

Fig. II-1. *To avoid jam-ups, stitch out from center of edge.*

Fig. II-2. *Shorten stitches rather than backstitching.*

❖ *Test any prospective edge-finishing method on scraps of your napkin fabric.* (Sorry, I had to tell you again.) Practice stitching on a 4" square, finishing the corner as you will the actual napkin. The five minutes spent testing will pay off with less sewing stress and more professional sewing.

❖ *Prevent jamming and stretching out an edge.* Some strategies:

♦ *Avoid stitching at a corner;* sew out from the center of an edge to the corners (Fig. II-1).

♦ *Rather than backstitching, shorten the stitch to 15/inch (15/2.5cm) for the first 3/8" (1cm).* See Fig. II-2.

♦ If the technique demands that you originate stitching at a corner, *hold and pull the thread tails to the back of the machine as you begin stitching* (Fig. II-3).

♦ *Start stitching on a tear-away nonwoven* (my favorite—see page 82) or two layers of water-soluble stabilizer; the foot will walk onto the fabric without jamming (Fig. II-4). Similarly, a "shim" can jam-proof stitching—use a credit card or similarly sized piece of cardboard under the back of the foot to smoothly feed stitching over the bulk of a corner (Fig. II-5).

(Commercial shims, such as the *Hump Jumper* and *Jean-a-ma-jig*™, are also sold; see "Handy Notions," page 81.)

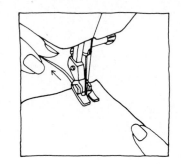

Fig. II-3. *At corners, pull threads as you begin to stitch.*

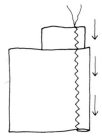

Fig. II-4. *Start stitching on tear-away wovens or layers of water-soluble stabilizer.*

Fig. II-5. *Use a "shim" for uniform feeding and stitching.*

♦ *Special feet can help ensure smooth feeding and minimize stretching*, such as a walking, even-feed or roller foot (see page 84).

❖ *Sew continuously* from napkin to napkin to minimize jamming at corners and to speed your production (Fig. II-6).

❖ *Watch your needle size and condition.* A too-dull or too-big needle can push the fabric into the throat plate hole, causing jamming.

❖ For smoothest feeding and pucker-free edges, remember: *For lighter-weight fabrics, shorten your stitch; for heavier fabrics, lengthen it.*

❖ Puckering a problem? *Holding the fabric taut under the foot as you sew* can also help eradicate unpredictable feeding and puckering (Fig. II-7).

❖ Stretching a problem? *Hold the fabric behind the presser foot with your index finger, while force-feeding the fabric under the foot* (called "ease plus"). This helps control stretching (Fig. II-8).

❖ If tunneling is a problem (when the fabric buckles as a zigzag or decorative stitch moves from left to right), *stabilize the fabric with tear-away nonwoven.* I find it indispensable, although better suited to lighter colors (sometimes all the nonwoven can't be torn away under the

stitch). *Other alternatives: Consider lining the napkin* (adding weight to the edge—see "6. Lined Napkins—in Minutes!", page 35), *or a using a special overcast or satin-edge foot* (see page 84).

❖ *Use a reputable brand of all-purpose polyester, cotton, or cotton-wrapped polyester thread*, unless a different thread is recommended. (Bargain-barrel threads can lack uniformity, causing stitch-tension and breakage problems.) Dig through your thread box and you'll undoubtedly find what you need—contrasting thread beautifully accents napkin edges and corners. Want a perfect match? Go for the shade that's slightly darker on the spool than your fabric.

❖ *To secure thread tails, dab on Fray Check™— the solution for anchoring the ends of satin stitching.*

❖ *Minimize bulk by trimming corners* as described for each napkin technique.

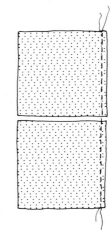

Fig. II-6. *For speed and jam-proofing, sew continuously.*

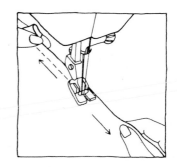

Fig. II-7. *Taut sew to prevent puckering.*

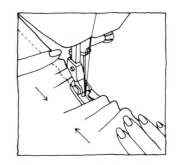

Fig. II-8. *Ease plus to prevent stretching.*

LINED NAPKINS—IN MINUTES!

—◆◆◆ **6** ◆◆◆—

*Here's a made-in-minutes
winner: surprisingly faster to
sew than many edge-finished
napkins and reversible, with
added body and absorbency.*

E A S Y - S E W ◆ T E C H N I Q U E

The Materials

❖ *Fabrics and linings shown here:* 50% cotton/50% polyester-blend stripe, print, and solid. Refer to "Fabric Credits," page 95. Or for both the fabric and lining, any light- to medium-weight wovens. (Lighter-weight combinations are more foldable.) Consider using a more absorbent unfinished cotton for the lining if the napkin layer is a nonabsorbent glazed fabric, such as chintz.

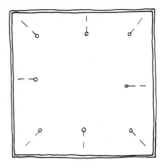

Fig 6-1. *Pin lining and napkin together.*

The Steps

1. Cut the fabric and lining squares the same size, allowing 3/8" (1 cm) seams on all sides.

2. Pin the lining to the napkin, right sides together. See Fig. 6-1 .

3. Using a medium-length straight stitch, sew the napkin and lining together, with a 3/8" (1cm) seam and leaving a 1-1/2" (4cm) opening for turning. Shorten to 15 stitches/inch (15/2.5cm) to secure the beginning and end of the stitching (Fig. 6-2).

   ### SMOOTH-TURNING TIP:

   Stitch diagonally across the corners, about 1 or 2 small stitches. See Fig. 6-2. The rounded corner will actually look more square than if stitched at a right angle.

Fig. 6-2. *Stitch together, sewing the corners diagonally; shorten stitches to secure seam ends.*

4. To minimize bulk, trim the allowances as shown (Fig. 6-2). Turn right side out, using a metal knitting needle or ruler to align the seamline at the napkin edge. To secure, edgestitch 1/8" (3mm) from the finished edge (Fig. 6-3).

OPTIONAL:

Topstitch an additional row 1/2" (1.3cm) from the finished edge. See Fig. 6-3 and the napkin shown at left.

The Fold

See the step-by-step folding how-to's for *6. Twin Peaks* on page 12.

Fig. 6-3. *Edgestitch. Optional: Topstitch, too.*

TWIN-NEEDLE TOPSTITCHED HEMS

◆◆◆ 7 ◆◆◆

*Twin-needle topstitching belies
the mere minutes spent
hemming: it's always perfectly
parallel and the zigzagged
bobbin thread discourages
raveling.*

EASY-SEW ◆ TECHNIQUE

The Materials

Fig. 7-1. *For twin-needle topstitching, spools should reel off in opposite directions.*

❖ **Fabrics shown here:** 100% cotton blue damask-look print, 50% cotton/50% polyester pink chintz, and 100% cotton ivory lace. Refer to "Fabric Credits," page 95. Or any light- to medium-weight, moderately to tightly constructed knit or woven.

❖ **Thread shown here:** 100% rayon thread.

❖ **Zigzag machine** that threads from the front to the back (enables use of a twin needle)

❖ **Twin needle:** one compatible in size with your fabric (see page 81).

The Steps

1. Cut out the napkin squares, allowing 1" (2.5cm) hems on all sides.

2. Thread the machine. Place the spools on the spool holders so that the thread strands reel off in opposite directions (Fig. 7-1).

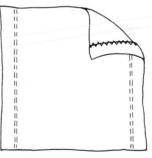

Fig. 7-2. *Fold up hem, twin-needle topstitch, and trim.*

3. Fold up a 1" (2.5cm) hem on one side. From the right side, twin-needle topstitch 3/4" (2cm) from the edge. On the wrong side, trim any excess hem allowance to the stitching. (The zigzag stitch formed on the bobbin side will effectively retard raveling.) See Fig. 7-2.

4. Working from opposite side to side, repeat for the other edges of the napkin (Fig. 7-3). On the last four corners, backstitch or shorten the stitch length to secure the topstitching; clip the thread tails close. See Fig. 7-4.

Fig. 7-3. *Working opposite side to side, hem, topstitch, and trim remaining edges.*

OPTIONAL:

Fold to miter the last four corners before twin-needle topstitching (Fig. 7-4).

VARIATIONS:

Vary the hem width. Also, try adjusting for a decorative machine stitch when twin-needle topstitching. See Fig. 7-4 and the lace napkin at left. *Caution:* Turn the handwheel to make sure the needles clear the foot plate.

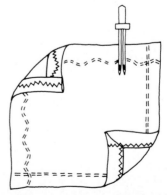

Fig. 7-4. *Optional: Fold to miter the last four corners before twin-needle topstitching. Variation: Adjust for decorative stitching when twin-needle topstitching.*

The Fold

See the step-by-step folding how-to's for **7. Flaming Flower** on page 13.

HEMMED AND SATIN-STITCHED EDGES

◆◆◆ 8 ◆◆◆

*When you want a beefier edge,
try this edge finish. Hemming
before satin stitching adds
body to the edges and
discourages tunneling
(buckling of the fabric under
the stitch).*

EASY-SEW ◆ TECHNIQUE

The Materials

❖ *Fabric shown here:* 100% cotton stripe and mini-floral prints. Refer to "Fabric Credits," page 95. Or any tightly woven fabric.

❖ *Thread shown here:* two strands of all-purpose thread in the needle—for better, faster coverage (one in the bobbin). Or any machine-embroidery or decorative thread (all-purpose weight or finer).

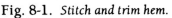

Fig. 8-1. *Stitch and trim hem.*

The Steps

1. Cut out the napkin squares, allowing at least 1/2" (1.3cm) hems on all sides.

2. Along one side, fold up a 1/2" (1.3cm) hem to the wrong side. Trim the corners in at an angle to decrease bulk. From the right side, straight stitch barely 1/8" (3mm) from the fold. Trim the hem allowance to the stitching. See Fig. 8-1.

   ### SMOOTH-SEWING TIPS:

   To prevent jam-ups, start stitching in the middle of an edge, stitching toward the corners. Also, change to a short straight-stitch for the last 1/2" (1.3cm), as shown. See Fig. 8-2.

3. From the right side, sew with a short satin-stitch zigzag width that covers the hem depth and the previous stitching (Fig. 8-2). Working from opposite side to side, repeat for the other sides. See Fig. 8-3.

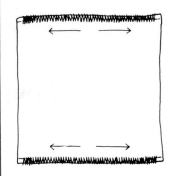

Fig. 8-2. *Satin stitch over hem, changing to a short straight stitch for the last 1/2" (1.3cm)*

VARIATIONS:

For an even beefier edge and more thread density, zigzag with a long, medium-width stitch instead of straight stitching (Step 2). Trim to the stitching and proceed with Step 3. Also, machine expert Jackie Dodson suggests turning up the hem, and from the right side, satin stitching over the fold *without straight stitching first or again* (Fig. 8-4); stitching over filler cord is optional.

Fig. 8-3. *Working opposite side to side, stitch, trim, and satin stitch the remaining edges.*

The Fold

See the step-by-step folding how-to's for *8. Simple Elegance* on page 13.

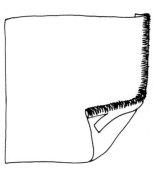

Fig. 8-4. *Variation: Satin stitch over fold and trim to stitching.*

Narrow Hems, Posthaste

◆◆ 9 ◆◆

*You don't need a fancy
machine or much time to
master this easy, lightweight
hem. Not pressing as you sew
(my apologies to all purists)
really saves time.*

EASY-SEW ◆ TECHNIQUE

The Materials

❖ *Fabrics shown here:* 100% cotton print, 50% cotton/50% polyester mint-green chintz. Refer to "Fabric Credits," page 95. Or any tightly woven, light- to medium-weight woven.

❖ *Thread shown here:* For the decorative-machine stitching on the mint-green napkin, 100% rayon thread. Or any all-purpose, embroidery, or decorative thread (all-purpose weight or lighter).

The Steps

1. Cut out the napkin squares, allowing 1/2" (1.3cm) hems on all sides.

2. Along one side, turn up a 1/4" (6mm) hem to the wrong side. Trim the corner to minimize bulk. Straight stitch 1/8" (3mm) from the fold. See Fig. 9-1.

   ### STITCH-LIKE-A-PRO TIPS:

   Longer stitches, 8 – 10/inch (3 – 4mm), look better because they float on the fabric surface, rather than burying themselves in the weave. Also, rather than backstitching to secure threads, simply shorten the stitch length.

3. Turn up 1/4" (6mm) again (Fig. 9-2). Straight stitch 1/8" (3mm) from the fold. (Jamming at the corners a problem? See page 32.) Working from opposite side to side, repeat for the other sides. See Fig. 9-3.

OPTIONAL:

Fold to miter the last four corners sewn (Fig. 9-3). For a folding-action illustration, see Fig. 14-6 on page 52.

VARIATION:

For the final hemming stitch (Step 3), utilize one of the many decorative-machine stitches found on most zigzag sewing machines. See Fig. 9-4 and the mint-green napkin at left.

The Fold

See the step-by-step folding how-to's for *9. Instant Drape* on page 13.

Fig. 9-1. *Trim corners, turn up 1/4" (6mm), and stitch.*

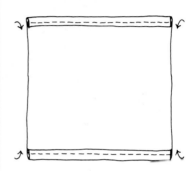

Fig. 9-2. *Turn up 1/4" (6mm) again and stitch.*

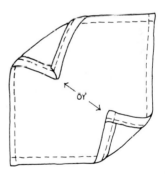

Fig. 9-3. *Working opposite side to side, repeat for remaining sides. Optional: Fold to miter corners before stitching.*

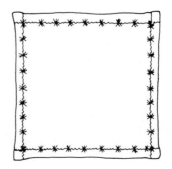

Fig. 9-4. *Variation: Hem with decorative machine stitch.*

DOUBLE SATIN-STITCHED EDGES

◆◆◆ 10 ◆◆

*Requiring only a basic zigzag-
model machine, this edge
finish is both decorative and
durable. Although I used
rayon thread here, any all-
purpose or machine-
embroidery thread works well.*

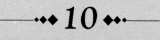

EASY-SEW ◆ TECHNIQUE

The Materials

- ❖ **Fabrics shown here**: 100% cotton, contrasting-color floral prints. Refer to "Fabric Credits," page 95. (For appliqué how-to's, see page 79.) Or any tightly constructed, light- to medium-weight woven.

- ❖ **Thread shown here**: 100% rayon thread. Or any all-purpose, machine-embroidery, or decorative thread (all-purpose weight or finer).

The Steps

1. Cut a fabric square for each napkin, adding a 1/2" (1.3cm) allowance on all sides. Mark and cut round corners (see page 74).

2. Using a narrow- to medium-width, medium-length zigzag, stitch 1/2" (1.3cm) from the edges (Fig. 10-1). Ease plus and/or stitch over tearaway nonwoven to minimize stretching (see page 32) and tunneling.

   ### TIMESAVING TIP:
   If you're making four or less napkins, you can cut the napkins out of the fabric after this step (Fig. 10-2).

3. With sharp scissors, trim to the stitching. Be careful not to cut the threads. See Fig. 10-1.

4. Satin-stitch with a slightly wider, shorter stitch directly over the first zigzag stitching. See Fig. 10-3.

VARIATIONS:

For added stability and edge definition, zigzag (Step 2) over filler, such as a strand of crochet thread or #5 pearl cotton. See Fig. 10-4. Or, for a heftier napkin with edges less prone to tunneling, fuse and satin stitch two fabric layers together (see Fig. 11-3, page 45), then zigzag, trim, and satin stitch.

The Fold

See the step-by-step folding how-to's for *10. Flying Ascot* on page 14.

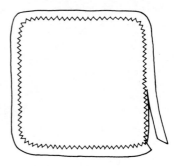

Fig. 10-1. *Zigzag and trim to stitching.*

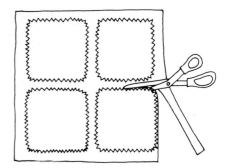

Fig. 10-2. *Optional: Cut out napkins after zigzagging (Step 2).*

Fig. 10-3. *Satin stitch over the first zigzag stitching.*

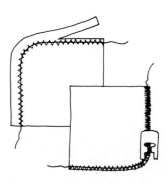

Fig. 10-4. *Variation: Zigzag over filler, then trim and satin stitch.*

DECORATIVELY MACHINE-STITCHED EDGES

◆◆ 11 ◆◆

*Bought a machine with lots of
neat decorative stitches, but
never use them? Here's your
chance...the stitch formation is
intriguing and the napkins are
lovely and very foldable.*

EASY-SEW ◆ TECHNIQUE

The Materials

❖ **Fabrics shown here:** 100% cotton, contrasting-color prints, fused together at the edges (see *Variations,* below). Refer to "Fabric Credits," page 95. Or for single-layer napkins, any crisp, stable, tightly woven medium- to heavy-weight fabric.

❖ **Thread shown here:** all-purpose sewing thread in the needle and the bobbin. Or any machine-embroidery or decorative thread (all-purpose weight or finer).

❖ **Sewing machine** with decorative satin-stitch capabilities. (Long scallops are favorites because trimming around the design isn't as tedious as trimming more intricate stitch motifs.)

Fig. 11-1. *Decoratively machine stitch around napkin.*

The Steps

1. Cut out the napkin squares, allowing 3/4" (2cm) hems on all sides. Mark and cut round corners (see page 74).

    ### DECORATIVE-STITCHING TIPS:

    Loosen the top tension so that the thread floats on top of the weave, and no bobbin thread is showing on the right side. Also, be careful not to stretch the edge as you sew (see page 33).

2. Starting in the middle of one side and 3/4" (2cm) from the edge, stitch around the napkin with a decorative stitch (Fig. 11-1).

3. Using sharp embroidery or appliqué scissors, trim to the stitching. Be careful not to clip the threads. See Fig. 11-2.

Fig. 11-2. *Carefully trim to stitching.*

VARIATIONS:

For extra body, line the napkins with self-fabric or a lighter-weight woven. For the firmest edges, fuse the fabric and lining layers together, using a 1-1/4" (3cm)-wide strip of fusible web (see page 19) sandwiched between. (Mark and round corners after fusing.) See Fig. 11-3. Finish the two layers as one, following Steps 2 and 3.

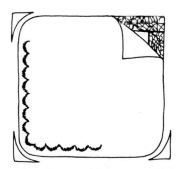

Fig. 11-3. *Variation: For firmer edges, fuse two layers together, decoratively machine stitch, and trim.*

The Fold

See the step-by-step folding how-to's for *11. Spiraled Fold-Up* on page 14.

EASY TRIMMED EDGES

◆◆◆ 12 ◆◆

*I love this napkin: the trim
parallels and accents the edge,
crisscrossing at the corners.
You'll marvel how easily the
trim is applied, with or
without a special foot.*

EASY-SEW ◆ TECHNIQUE

The Materials

❖ *Fabrics shown here:* 100% cotton contemporary prints. Refer to "Fabric Credits," page 95. Or any moderately to tightly woven, light- to medium-weight fabric.

❖ *Trim shown here:* 100% polyester, 3/8" (1cm)-wide grosgrain ribbon. Or any 1/8" – 3/8" (3mm – 1cm)-wide *prewashed* flat trim or ribbon. You'll need the finished napkin perimeter measurement plus 4" (10cm). For instance, for an 18" (46cm) finished napkin, you'll need 2-1/8 yards (1.9 meters) of trim.

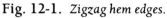

Fig. 12-1. *Zigzag hem edges.*

The Steps

1. Cut out the napkin squares, allowing 1-1/4" (3cm) hems on all sides. Cut the trim for each napkin into four equal lengths.

2. Along one side, fold up a 1-1/4" (3cm) hem to the wrong side. From the wrong side, zigzag along the raw hem edge. See Fig. 12-1. Repeat for the other side.

3. From the right side, cover the zigzagging with the trim; edgestitch in place. See Fig. 12-2. Trim off any excess trim.

4. On the remaining pair of edges, fold up 1-1/4" (3cm) hems. Zigzag the hems in place, starting and stopping at the trim, as shown. Then fold under the last four corners to form the miters (Fig. 12-3). On the right side, cover the zigzagging with the trim, allowing equal-length extensions and sandwiching the trim ends between the folded miters and the hems. (Use gluestick or permanent glue to position the trim.) Edgestitch the trim in place. See Fig. 12-4.

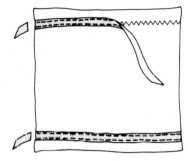

Fig. 12-2. *Cover zigzagging with trim; edgestitch.*

VARIATIONS:

To decoratively stitch the trim in place, use twin-needle topstitching, blindhemming, or tri-motion rickrack stitching.

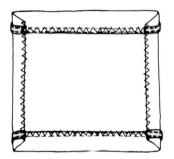

Fig. 12-3. *On remaining opposite sides, zigzag hems as shown and fold miters before edgestitching trim.*

The Fold

See the step-by-step folding how-to's for *12. Easy Roll-Up, Tied or Ringed* on page 14.

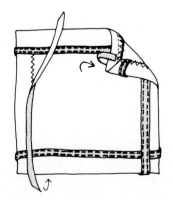

Fig. 12-4. *Tuck trim ends under miters and edgestitch trim.*

HIDDEN-SEAM TRIM FINISH

◆◆ 13 ◆◆

*With this simple trim
application, edges can't ravel,
and the back of the napkin
looks nearly as good as the
front. The trim-bordered edges
accent any table setting,
beautifully.*

EASY-SEW ◆ TECHNIQUE

The Materials

❖ *Fabrics and linings shown here:* 100% cotton holiday prints (see *Variations*, below). Refer to "Fabric Credits," page 95. Or any moderately to tightly woven, light- to medium-weight woven.

❖ *Trims shown here:* 100% cotton print, extracted from the holiday print (see *Variations*, below—press under 1/4" (6mm)-width allowances on each side of the stripe). Or any prewashed finished-edge trim or ribbon, any width desired, although generally 1/2" to 1-1/2" (1.3cm to 4cm) wide. You'll need 2-1/8 yards (1.9 meters) of 1" (2.5cm)-wide trim for each 18" (46cm) unfinished napkin.

Fig. 13-1. *Lap trim and edgestitch.*

The Steps

1. Cut out napkin squares, allowing 1/4" (6mm) hems on all sides. Cut the trim as you apply it to each edge.

2. Lap the trim 1/4" (6mm) over the wrong side of one edge, 1/4" (6mm) (or half the trim width) short of the beginning and end of the side, as shown. Edgestitch in place (Fig. 13-1). Press to the right side, aligning the trim along the edge. Repeat for the opposite side (Fig. 13-2). Edgestitch the other side of the trim. (To flatten wider trims, edgestitch again, over the first stitching line, through the trim and the napkin.)

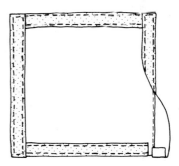

Fig. 13-2. *Align trim along edge and edgestitch.*

3. On the remaining pair of opposite sides: Lap the trim 1/4" (6mm) over the edge, allowing 1/2" (1.3cm) extensions at each end. Edgestitch. Press to the right side, aligning the trim along the edge. Before edgestitching the other side of the trim, tuck in the extensions even with the intersecting edge. (Trim as necessary to reduce bulk.) Edgestitch in place, including the trim ends (Fig. 13-3).

VARIATIONS

For more body and reversibility, line the napkin. For perfectly matching trim, extract a stripe from the napkin fabric (see photograph, left). For a fringed and larger-looking napkin, substitute purchased fringe for the trim or ribbon (Fig. 13-4); in Step 2 (above), lap the fringe trim over the right side.

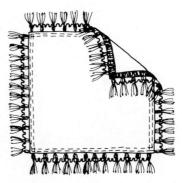

Fig. 13-3. *Tuck under trim extensions and edgestitch.*

The Fold

See the step-by-step folding how-to's for *13. Napkin Nosegay* on page 15.

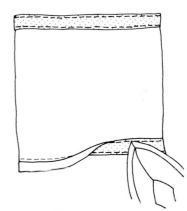

Fig. 13-4. *Variation: Use purchased fringe for trim.*

No-Measure Miters

— ◆◆ 14 ◆ —

*This happens to be the best
mitering technique I know of,
perfect for napkins, hankies,
scarves, and just about any
corner that demands neatness.*

EASY-SEW ◆ TECHNIQUE

The Materials

❖ *Fabrics and lining shown here:* 100% cotton, contrasting-color brush-stroke prints and 50% rayon/50% polyester burgundy solid. Refer to "Fabric Credits," page 95. With the exception of very soft fabrics, just about any fabric, woven or knit, will work well. (If a reversible fabric is used, or one without a discernible right or wrong side, the mitered hems can be turned to the right side.)

The Steps

1. Carefully cut out napkin squares on grain, allowing 1" (2.5cm) hems on all sides (or any hem depth desired, plus 3/8" or 1cm).

2. Mark the hemlines (see page 74), making sure the depths are uniform throughout. See Fig. 14-1.

3. Fold the corner right sides together, so that the raw edges align. Fold the corner again, as shown, aligning all the raw edges. See Fig. 14-2. Using the diagonal foldline as a guide, straight stitch next to (but not catching) the fold; to avoid jamming, start 3/8" (1cm) in from the raw edges and stitch toward the corner point. Shorten the stitch to secure the seam ends. See Fig. 14-3.

4. Trim the seam, tapering at the corner to minimize bulk. Finger press the trimmed seam open, and turn right side out. Center the miter. See Fig. 14-3.

5. Repeat for the other corners.

6. Turn under the raw edges 3/8" (1cm), press, and topstitch (Fig. 14-4), being careful to stitch a uniform distance (1/2" – 5/8" or 1.3 – 1.5cm) from the hemline fold.

VARIATIONS:

Finish the edges first (before Step 2), with zigzagging, overlock stitching, or, if using a tightly constructed fabric, pinking. Then topstitch the hem (Step 6) without turning the hem edge under. See Fig. 14-5.

The Fold

See the step-by-step folding how-to's for *14. Double-Point Pocket* on page 15.

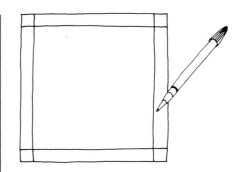

Fig. 14-1. *Mark uniform-depth hemlines.*

Fig. 14-2. *Fold, aligning raw edges. Fold corner again, aligning raw edges.*

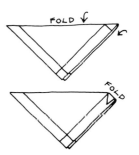

Fig. 14-3. *Starting 3/8" (1cm) in from raw edges, stitch toward corner.*

Fig. 14-4. *Turn under edges and topstitch.*

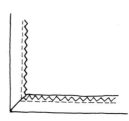

Fig. 14-5. *Variations: Zigzag, serge, or pink edges, then topstitch.*

For Napkins Made or Ready-Made: No-Sew Embellishments I

❖ *Fuse-and-paint-on appliqués.* For appliqué amateurs (as I am), the best, fastest and most professional method utilizes a cut-out from a printed fabric, such as a flower cut from a medium-to-large scale print.

1. First, fuse fusible transfer web (see page 19) to the wrong side of the printed fabric (Fig. II-9). Allow to cool and dry. Then carefully cut out the flower appliqué(s) (Fig. II-10).

2. Peel the paper backing off, position on the napkin (a corner is generally best) and fuse in place (Fig. II-11).

3. After the fusing has cooled, lay the wrong side of the napkin over a paper-protected work area. Outline sparingly with fabric paints around the appliqué edges, brushing to smooth and feather the paint if you like. See Fig. II-12. (Practice to avoid applying ugly paint globs.)

❖ *Paint-on designs.* Either fake it with stencils, enhance an iron-on, or go for it free-hand.

❖ *Glue-on flat, prewashed trim.* Mark trim lines on the right side of the napkin using washable marking pen or a chalk wheel. Apply permanent glue (see page 18) to the wrong side of flat, flexible trim or ribbon and stick to the napkin, turning under the raw ends of the trim. See Fig. II-13.

LEARN-FROM-MY-MISTAKES TIP:

After application, allow the fabric paints and glue overnight drying time. If corners of your appliqués come up, use permanent glue to tack down. Also, protect painted napkins by laundering and drying in a pillow case, and by pressing face down on a soft cloth, from the wrong side.

Fig. II-11. *Peel paper backing off, position, and fuse.*

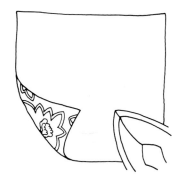

Fig. II-9. *Fuse transfer web to wrong side of fabric.*

Fig. II-12. *Outline appliqué edges with fabric paint.*

Fig. II-10. *Carefully cut out appliqué.*

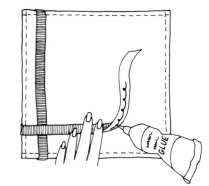

Fig. II-13. *Glue on flat, prewashed trim.*

Napkinmaking As Never Before: Sensational Serged Edges

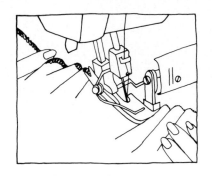

Fig. III-1. *Ease-plus to prevent stretching.*

❖ *Know that you are justified in buying a serger for the single purpose of making napkins. I similarly reassured several friends. Each one bought a serger, all are madly serging napkins, and not one is experiencing buyer's remorse.*

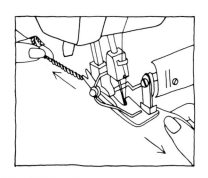

Fig. III-2. *Taut serge to prevent puckering.*

❖ *I promise this is the last time I'll say it* (maybe—at least in this book): *test edge-finishing on the crosswise and lengthwise scraps* of the same fabric. You'll notice a difference in how the grainlines should be handled; typically, the lengthwise grain is more stable but can be prone to puckering (use taut serging), whereas the crosswise grain tends to stretch (use ease-plus). Uncertain which is which? The crosswise grain threads are slightly heavier and generally easier to unravel than those running lengthwise.

❖ *Utilize varied feed techniques.* For ease-plussed serging, to prevent stretching of less stable fabrics and edges, dial between or to "1" and the highest (usually "2") setting, which means a 2:1 feeding ratio. To simulate this easing action by hand: hold the fabric behind the presser foot with your index finger, while force-feeding the fabric under the foot (Fig. III-1).

For taut serging, to prevent puckering of lightweight or single-layer fabric (especially when serging a narrow rolled edge), dial the lowest (usually ".7") setting, which means a .7:1 feeding ratio. To simulate this pulling action by hand: hold the fabric edge taut in front of and behind the presser foot (Fig. III-2).

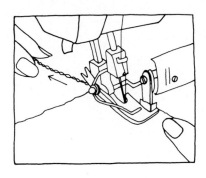

Fig. III-3. *To prevent stitching jam-up at edge, pull thread chain.*

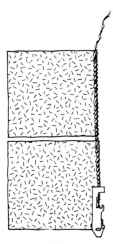

Fig. III-4. *To save time and prevent jamming, serge continuously.*

❖ To prevent jamming and stretching out an edge, **hold and pull the thread chain to the back of the machine** as you begin stitching (Fig. III-3). Serging continuously from one napkin to another gives you a good handle for this pulling action and speeds your production (Fig. III-4).

❖ For smoothest feeding and pucker-free edges, *follow these general stitch length rules:* for lighter-weight fabrics and threads, shorten your stitch; for heavier fabrics and threads lengthen it.

❖ *Use any reputable brand of serger or all-purpose polyester, cotton, or cotton-wrapped polyester thread,* unless a different thread is recommended. (Threads of inconsistent quality can cause thread tension and breakage problems.) Remember that the loopers are the threads that show. So, if you've got three spools of thread, one of which is a shade or too off, don't worry—use that for the needle. For better thread covering, use two all-purpose or serger threads in each of the upper and lower loopers (so you will need five spools or cones and two additional thread holders—see page 83).

❖ If your narrow rolled or unrolled edges are pulling off, *lengthen the stitch length, widen the stitch bite (consult your manual or dealer), and/or*

decrease the needle size. Also, try serge-finishing the lengthwise edges first, then the crosswise edges; the lengthwise grain has less tendency to pull out where the serging intersects.

❖ If fabric threads are poking out between the serged stitches, *shorten the stitch length, widen the stitch bite (again, consult your manual or dealer) and/or use woolly (multifilament) stretch nylon in the looper(s).* Also, try serging over water-soluble stabilizer such as *Solvy* or *Wash-Away Plastic Stabilizer*—it neatens rolled edge when nothing else does.

❖ *Use seam sealant such as Fray Check™ to secure threads at corners.*

❖ *Decrease bulk by trimming corners* as described for each napkin technique.

❖ *Remember that serge-finishing napkins is the perfect beginner's project;* set up the machine and watch them marvel at the edge transformation. My daughter, Bett, willingly volunteers for the "job" of serging napkin edges. Any major mistakes are reserged smaller to become doll napkins and scarves.

SIMPLE: SERGED, TURNED, & TOPSTITCHED

—◆◆ 15 ◆◆—

*The K.I.S.S. (Keep it simple,
silly) principle never fails me,
and this finish is just that:
simple. (Not to mention that it
passes the triple "F" test—
fast, flat, and foldable.)*

SERGED ◆ TECHNIQUE

The Materials

❖ *Fabrics shown here:* 100% cotton tapestry-look print and teal-green solid. Refer to "Fabric Credits," page 95. Or just about any fabric, woven or knit.

The Steps

SERGER SETTINGS:

Adjust for a medium-width, medium-length, balanced 2- or 3-thread stitch.

1. Cut out napkin squares, allowing 3/4" (2cm) hems on all sides (or any hem depth desired plus 1/4" (6mm) (although I prefer this finish relatively narrow).

2. Serge-finish all the edges, trimming 1/4" (6mm) throughout (Fig. 15-1).

3. Turn up one side 3/8" (1 cm); trim the corners as shown to decrease bulk. Using your sewing machine, from the wrong side, topstitch the hem about 1/4" (6mm) from the fold. Repeat for the opposite side. See Fig. 15-2.

4. Repeat Step 3 for the other pair of opposite sides, but do not trim the corners. See Fig. 15-3.

VARIATION:

A decorative edge can be created if lighter-weight or soft fabric is used and the hem is decoratively blindstitched. You will work with the bulk of the napkin on the right. (Robbie Fanning tells me that a shell stitch, available on many machines, will achieve the same look but the napkin bulk remains to the left, as in usual sewing.) Adjust for the widest stitch possible and allow the zigzag portion of the stitch to barely fall off the hem. See Fig. 15-4.

The Fold

See the step-by-step folding how-to's for *15. Soft Folds in a Ring* on page 15.

Fig. 15-1. *Serge-finish edges.*

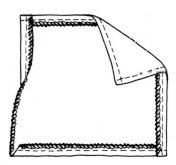

Fig. 15-2. *Turn up, trim, and topstitch hem. Repeat for opposite side.*

Fig. 15-3. *On the remaining sides, turn and topstitch hems (do not trim).*

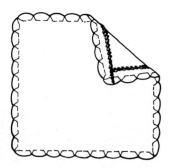

Fig. 15-4. *Variation: Use a machine blindstitch for topstitching.*

NARROW ROLLED-EDGE FINISH

◆◆ 16 ◆◆

*Before home-use sergers, only
factory-made napkins were
finished with narrow rolled
edging. Now in mere minutes,
you, too, can finish edges with
this elegant, lightweight stitch.*

S E R G E D ◆ T E C H N I Q U E

The Materials

❖ *Fabrics shown here:* 100% cotton, Imari-inspired prints (a round motif was extracted for the unfolded napkin). Refer to "Fabric Credits," page 95. Or any light- to medium-weight woven. Avoid loosely woven, stiff, or heavy fabrics, because the edges resist rolling.

❖ *Threads shown here: upper looper*—one strand of metallic rayon and one strand of 100% rayon thread; *lower looper*—woolly stretch nylon (to enhance rolling—see "Handy Notions," page 83); *needle*—all-purpose serger thread.

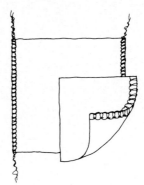

Fig. 16-1. *Serge-finish lengthwise edges. Close-up: Narrow-rolled edge finish.*

The Steps

SERGER SETTINGS:

Adjust for a narrow rolled hemming (consult your serger owner's manual) and a short stitch length (1.0 – 1.5mm). Tighten the lower looper (of a 3-thread stitch) or the needle (of a 2-thread stitch) to form a straight line on the underside of the stitch. (For a close-up of the stitch, see Fig. 16-1.) Refer to pages 56 for solutions to puckering problems.

1. Cut out napkin squares, allowing 1/4" (6mm) hems on all sides.

2. Serge-finish all the edges (usually the stronger lengthwise grain first), trimming 1/4" (6mm) throughout. Rounding corners slightly will prevent them from becoming too pointed; angle in about 1/8" (3mm) for the last 1/2" (1.3cm) or so and start the next edge in about 1/8" (3mm), then angle out. See Fig. 16-2.

3. Dab seam sealant (see page 83) sparingly on each corner, allow to dry, and trim the thread tails (Fig. 16-2).

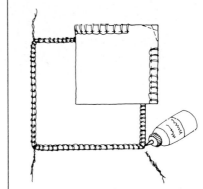

Fig. 16-2. *Serge-finish crosswise edges; angle in and out from corners.*

VARIATIONS:

Line with a coordinating or contrasting fabric and serge-finish as one layer. If feasible, moderate the crosswise stretching problem and ensure stitch uniformity by aligning them with the lengthwise grain of lining pieces. See Fig. 16-3. To facilitate continuous serging, round off corners before finishing (Fig. 16-4) or cut out round napkins (see page 74).

Fig. 16-3. *Variation: Line napkin, alternating grain directions to control edge stretch.*

The Fold

See the step-by-step folding how-to's for *16. Soft, Quick Candlestick* on page 16.

Fig. 16-4. *Round off corners to serge continuously.*

UNROLLED-EDGE FINISH

✦✦ 17 ✦✦

*When you've got a fabric that
resists rolling, want a slightly
wider, flatter edge, or need a
reversible stitch, serge-finish
the edges unrolled, evenly
balancing the looper tensions.*

SERGED ◆ TECHNIQUE

The Materials

❖ *Fabrics shown here:* 100% cotton, metallic-paisley prints. Refer to "Fabric Credits," page 95. Or any light- to medium-weight, woven cotton or cotton blend. Avoid loosely woven fabrics, because the edges will stretch out or the serged finish may pull off.

❖ *Threads shown here:* upper looper—one strand of rayon metallic and one strand of all-purpose thread (for better coverage); *lower looper*—one strand of heavy metallic-fleck thread; *needle*—one strand of all-purpose thread. Or, for the loopers, any weight or thread or combination of threads that will achieve the look and coverage desired. For better edge coverage, try topstitching thread, or two strands of all-purpose, serger, or woolly stretch nylon thread in the loopers.

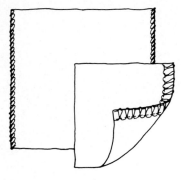

Fig. 17-1. *Working opposite side to side, serge-finish all edges.* **Close-up:** Unrolled *edge finish.*

The Steps

SERGER SETTINGS:

Adjust to the desired width in a balanced, 2- or 3-thread stitch (Fig.17-1); consult your owner's manual. Adjust the stitch length to optimize thread coverage.

1. Cut out napkin squares, allowing 1/4" (6mm) hems on all sides.

2. Working opposite side to side, serge-finish all the edges, trimming 1/4" (6mm) throughout (Fig. 17-2). Rounding corners slightly will prevent them from becoming too pointed. See Fig. 16-2 on page 61.

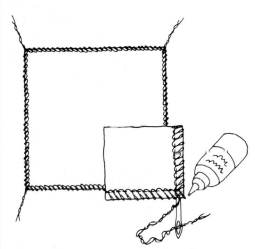

Fig. 17-2. *Bury thread tails and/or use seam sealant.*

   ### TIMESAVING TIP:

   When using heavier decorative threads, leave ample thread tails (at least 3" or 7.5cm long) when you start and finish serge-finishing the last two pair of edges. With a tapestry needle or knit picker (see page 83), the tails can be buried neatly under the stitch to secure the serging, eliminating the need to turn corners. See Fig. 17-2.

3. If using serger, all-purpose, or woolly stretch nylon thread, don't worry about burying the thread tails: dab seam sealant (see page 83) sparingly on each corner, allow to dry, and trim the thread tails.

VARIATIONS:

For a heftier edge, fold under 1/2" (1.3cm) before serge-finishing. Trim to the serging. See Fig. 17-3. To facilitate continuous serge-finishing, round corners (see Fig. 16-4 on page 61 and the napkin at left).

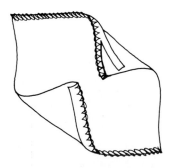

Fig. 17-3. *Variation: For a heftier edge, fold under 1/2" (1.3cm), serge-finish, and trim to stitching.*

The Fold

See the step-by-step folding how-to's for **17.** *Spiral* on page 16.

LAPPED-TRIM FINISH

◆◆◆ 18 ◆◆◆

*On this napkin, ravel-proof
serging finishes the fabric
edge, so the trim can be lapped
and edgestitched without bulky
seaming. Voilà, a trimmed
edge that's flat and foldable.*

SERGED ◆ TECHNIQUE

The Materials

❖ **Fabrics shown here:** 100% cotton metallic prints. Refer to "Fabric Credits," page 95. Or just about any napkin-like fabric, knit or woven.

❖ **Trims shown here:** 100% polyester, 1-1/2" (4cm)-wide black/metallic (ribbon) and 100% polyester, 1" (2.5cm)-wide red satin ribbon (serge-finished along both edges with narrow rolled edging and metallic threads). Or any prewashed trim, from 3/4" (2cm) to 2" (5cm) wide. You'll need the unfinished napkin perimeter measurement plus nine times the trim width. For an 18" (46cm) unfinished napkin and 1" (2.5cm)-wide trim, you'll need 72" (1.8 meters) plus 9" (23cm) or about 2-1/4 yards (2 meters) of trim.

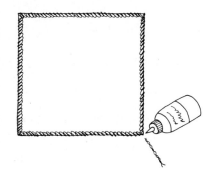

Fig. 18-1. *Serge-finish all edges; secure corner threads with seam sealant.*

The Steps

SERGER SETTINGS:

Adjust for medium-width, medium-length, balanced 2-, 3-, or 3/4-thread serged finishing.

1. Cut out napkin squares, allowing 1/4" (6mm) hems on all sides. Cut the trim to length after aligning on each edge (see Steps 3 and 4).

2. Serge-finish all sides of the napkin, trimming 1/4" (6mm). Secure the corner threads with seam sealant; trim the thread tails. See Fig. 18-1.

Fig. 18-2. *Lap and edgestitch trim, folding to miter corners.*

3. Lap the trim 1/4" (6mm) over the right side of one edge, completely covering the serging (Fig. 18-2). With your sewing machine, edgestitch, folding to miter the corners, as shown (Fig. 18-3).

4. Edgestitch the miters in place. Trim the seams to the edge stitching.

The Fold

See the step-by-step folding how-to's for *18. Napkin Knot-in-no-Time* on page 16.

Fig. 18-3. *Edgestitch and trim miters.*

FOR NAPKINS MADE OR READY-MADE: NO-SEW EMBELLISHMENTS II

❖ *Iron-on foils, decals, and letters.* Visit your nearest craft or fabric store. You'll be amazed by the selection. Iron-ons may be more vivid on a synthetic or synthetic/cotton-blends than on 100% cotton; test on fabric scraps.

❖ *Take advantage of computer technology.* Wax thermal-based (not xerographic-based) high-quality color printers can now print out on iron-on transfer paper, in color. (For printing and paper sources, ask your local computer dealer or look up "Computer Services" and "Desktop Publishing" in the Yellow Pages. One paper supplier, Biflyx Photowear, will sell this type of thermal-transfer paper, but their minimum is $97 —about $1 per 8-1/2" x 11" sheet; contact them at 714/539-7180.) Following the paper manufacturer's how-to's, iron onto the napkin. *Warning:* The computer print-outs I've worked with require a hot, dry iron and the paper must be pulled off the fabric while it is still warm.

Also, note that there are special ribbons available for dot-matrix printers, that, when printed on regular paper, can be ironed onto fabric.

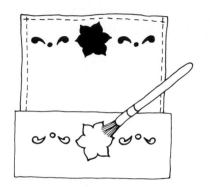

Fig. III-5. *Stencil or stamp on paper or fabric napkins.*

Fig. III-6. *Let kids decorate paper napkins.*

❖ *Stencil and stamp on paper or fabric napkins* (Fig. III-5). Practice on waste paper first to perfect your technique. For fabric napkins, select permanent inks and allow to set overnight before using or laundering.

❖ *Let kids decorate their own napkins.* Younger children can stencil, stamp, or draw with crayons on paper napkins (Fig. III-6), a great activity for a birthday party.

NAPKINS DO DOUBLE-DUTY

IV

◆

Napkins as Gift Wrap

◆

Napkin Ideas Around the House

◆

Napkins as Pillows

Napkins As Gift Wrap

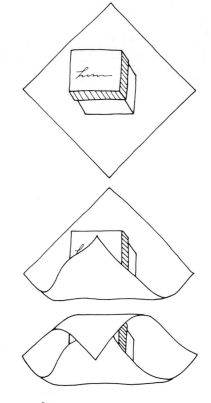

❖ *Why not copy the Japanese furoshiki? Wrap gifts, goodies, and shopping booty in squares of fabric, also known as napkins.*

Fig. IV-1. *Wrapped-and-tied gift wrap.*

Tying tip:

TYING TIP:

For those wraps that tie, use unlined light- to medium-weight napkins with lightweight narrow-hem or edge finishing. The larger the napkin, the more wrapping and tying versatility. A 20" (51cm)-square napkin wraps and ties nicely around a 9" (23cm)-wide, 7" (18cm)-long, 2" (5cm)-deep box. When you don't have a suitable napkin on hand, substitute other squares: scarves, large hankies, or bandannas.

❖ *Wrapped-and-tied gift wrap.* Center your gift on the wrong side of the napkin. The more symmetrical the box, the more even the wrap and tie.) Fold two opposite corners over the top. Securing with a safety pin is optional, although suggested if a durably snug fit is desired. Bring the remaining corners over the top. Tie, twist, and hide the corners under the folds. Or tie in a more secure square knot, leaving the corners exposed, or tucking them under the folds. See Fig. IV-1 and the back cover.

GIFT-GIVING TIP:

Wrap a set of napkins with one of the set. Fold all but one of the napkins into sixteenths and stack neatly. With the leftover napkin, wrap the stack into a soft package, as described above. See Fig. IV-2.

Fig IV-2. *Gift wrap napkin set with a napkin from the set.*

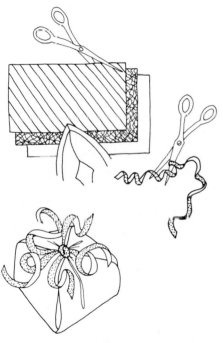

Fig. IV-3. *Fuse fabric to gift wrap, cut into strips, curl, and tuck under napkin knot.*

TRIMMING TIP:

Make coordinating fabric/ribbon curls that can be slipped under the tie. Fuse fusible transfer web (see page 19) to the napkin fabric. Peel off the transfer web paper and fuse to paper gift wrap. Cut into 1/2" – 3/4" (1.3 – 2cm) bias strips and curl with scissors on the fabric side. See Fig. IV-3 and the back cover.

❖ *Ten-second tie-ups.* Simply center the gift on the wrong side of the napkin and tie hobo-style, or tie up with ribbon, cording, or trim (Fig. IV-4).

❖ *It's-a-wrap! bottle cover.* Center your bottle on the wrong side of the napkin. (For a standard wine bottle, use a 20" (51cm) or larger napkin. Smaller napkins can be used for proportionately smaller bottles.) Bring the two corners from one side up, crisscross wrapping around the neck of the bottle. Bring the remaining corners up and around the neck of the bottle, covering the previous wrapping. Tie in a loose square knot to create a soft handle for carrying. See Fig. IV-5.

Fig. IV-4. *Tie up gifts with napkins and ribbons.*

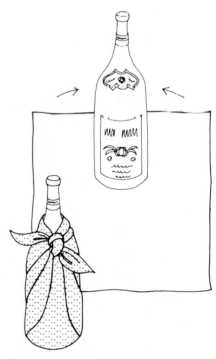

Fig. IV-5. *Use napkin to wrap and carry bottle.*

NAPKIN IDEAS AROUND THE HOUSE

❖ *These ideas should convince you: Napkins are much more than just dining-table accents. Have fun sprucing up your living and working environment with a few napkins and very little time or money.*

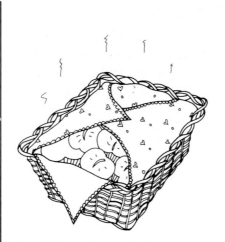

❖ **Fold as a bun cover/warmer.** The napkin should be at least 15" (38cm) square, preferably 20"+ (51cm+), depending on the size of your buns.

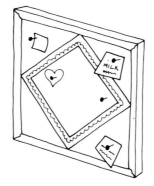

❖ **Perk up a blah bulletin board.**

❖ *Line or tie around a basket.*

❖ **Position as placemats.**

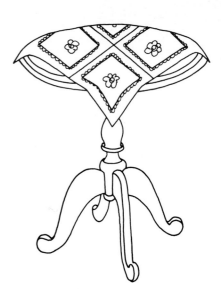

❖ *Tape together to temporarily form table toppings.* Diagonal arrangements are particularly appealing. (Use wide transparent-type tape on the wrong sides to "seam" the napkins together).

❖ **Lap diagonally to form a table runner.**

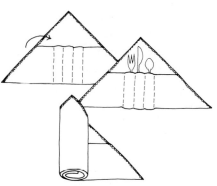

❖ *Make "Lapkins."* (An inspiration from my friend and fellow author, Jan Saunders.) Fold and channel stitch a reversible napkin to form pockets for silverware.

❖ *Arrange as chair tidies*. Upholstery pins pushed in and safely hidden between cushions or double-sided tape will help them stay put. On stools, tie on with ribbons or cording.

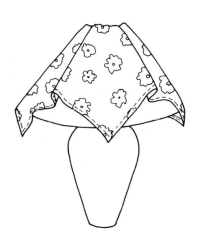

❖ *Slipcover a lampshade.* (Be careful that the napkin doesn't touch the bulb.)

❖ *Drape one or more over a rod as a no-sew, reusable valance.* Tape or pin to prevent slippage.

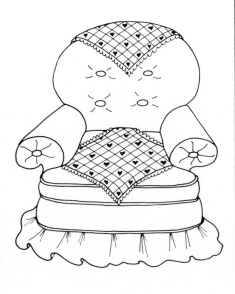

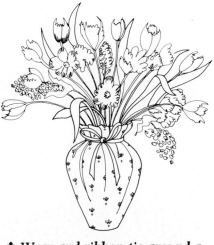

❖ *Wrap and ribbon-tie around a vase*. Similarly wrapped vases are selling in New York florist shops for $90.

NAPKINS AS PILLOWS

Fig. IV-6. *Lap and handstitch over a pillow.*

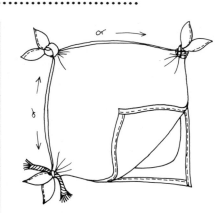

Fig. IV-8. *Knot, tie, or wrap napkin corners to cover a pillow.*

❖ *Add napkin accents.*
(A wonderful way to coordinate pillows in a kitchen-seating area.) Sandwich a pillow between the wrong sides of two napkins. Lap the napkin corners as shown (Fig. IV-6) and hand tack in place.

❖ *Edgestitch two napkins together* to make a pillow or pillow cover. If the napkin is larger than the pillow or form, topstitch in from the edge to create a flange. See Fig. IV-7.

❖ *Instantly slipcover a worn or outdated pillow* or uninteresting muslin-covered pillow form. Place the form between the wrong sides of two napkins. If the napkins are considerably larger than the pillow, knot the corners together to form the cover. If the napkins are only slightly larger than the pillow, use rubber bands, soutache braid, or decorative cording to tie the corners. See Fig. IV-8. If the napkins are tied right sides together, the ties will be hidden when the cover is turned right sides out (Fig. IV-9).

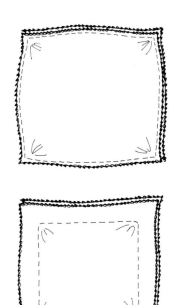

Fig. IV-7. *Edgestitch napkins together to make a pillow or pillow cover.*

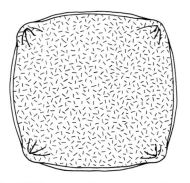

Fig. IV-9. *Tie right sides together and turn to hide ties.*

THE NAPKINMAKERS'
TIME-AND-MONEY-SAVING GUIDE

FASTEST MARKING AND CUTTING OUT

❖ *Consider all the cutting options.* Alter the unfinished size slightly, up or down, to maximize the napkin yield (see pages 85-91) and to minimize waste. Also, don't rule out bias-grain or round napkins. (A wok lid is the perfect template when making round napkins. See Fig. V-1.)

❖ For fastest (and most enjoyable) marking and cutting out, *use a gridded large cutting mat; a wide, long ruler; T- or L-square; and rotary cutter* (Fig. V-2).

❖ *Avoid marking,* if possible. If using a loosely woven fabric, a check, plaid, or stripe, *eyeball cutting lines, using the crosswise or lengthwise yarns as cutting guides* (Fig. V-3). Cut the fabric into crosswise napkin-width strips, then cut into napkins along the lengthwise yarns.

Or try using a cardboard or acrylic template of the unfinished napkin size, as another marking alternative. Using a coffee cup as a marking guide, round the corners of the template, if the napkin style so requires. Then rotary cut around the templates. See Fig. V-4.

Finally, if the fabric isn't a knit or tightly woven, you can *pull threads to mark* for cutting in the crosswise direction, then measure the lengthwise direction cuts (lengthwise threads are more stubborn,

resisting pulling). Pull the thread only as far as it pulls easily and cut. Then ravel another thread and repeat the process. See Fig. V-5.

❖ If you must mark (preferably on the wrong side), use a washable, *water-soluble or vanishing marking pen, light pencil, or chalk wheel.* See page 81.

❖ *Refrain from tearing;* puckered pull lines radiate from the torn edges. I must admit I've torn napkins before: when in doubt, test first.

❖ *Don't pray over grainlines.* Sure, it's preferable to parallel the lengthwise and crosswise grainlines precisely, but straying off somewhat won't show on the finished napkin.

❖ To uniformly round corners on napkins already cut out, *fold and cut the napkin in fourths.* Then, using a coffee cup as a marking guide, rotary cut through all layers in a way similar to Fig. V-4.

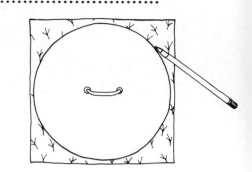

Fig V-1. *A large wok lid works well as a round napkin template.*

Fig. V-2. *For fastest cutting out, use a gridded cutting mat, long ruler, and rotary cutter.*

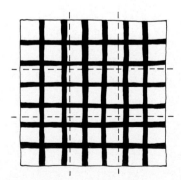

Fig. V-3. *Use plaid or stripe lines as cutting guides.*

FAVORITE NAPKIN FABRICS

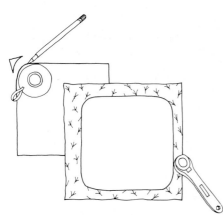

Fig. V-4. *Cutting option: Rotary cut around cardboard or acrylic template.*

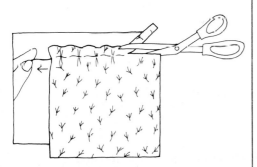

Fig. V-5. *Marking/cutting option for wovens: pull threads.*

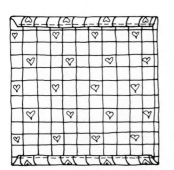

Fig. V-6. *Cut, hem, and stitch along stripe, check, and plain lines.*

❖ *Stripes, checks, and plaids.* What could be easier and more accurate to cut out and make? You've got premarked cutting and hemming lines, woven in (Fig. V-6).

❖ *Reversibles.* On fabric-store flat-fold tables everywhere, you will find discounted double-sided cottons (Fig. V-7). It's a challenge to conjure up garment ideas for these puzzling reversibles, but napkins are a cinch.

❖ *Real linen.* The elegance and foldability are unsurpassed.

❖ *Napkin-square cutouts.* Printed in a square, the printed corners are "mitered" for you (Fig. V-8). (Now that's what I call easy.) For a heftier napkin, I frequently line with the coordinating all-over print.

❖ *Exotic prints.* Wild, large-scale prints have always attracted me, but have limited purposefulness in my wardrobe. Whether wovens or knits, they're perfect for napkins.

❖ *Flat sheets.* When 20 or more napkins are needed, I consider flat sheets. The cost each is only $1 for the twenty 20" (51cm) napkins you'll yield from a $20 double flat sheet (see "Napkin Yields for Flat Sheets," page 93).

❖ *"Silver" linings.* Soften the straight lines of checks and plaids by lining them with florals (Fig. V-9). Or pick a bright contrast to a muted or dark shade.

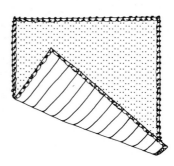

Fig. V-7. *Reversibles—easy to finish, lovely to fold.*

Fig. V-8. *Easiest cutting out—napkin-square prints.*

Fig. V-9. *Use linings to add color, print accents, weight, and/or absorbency.*

FIBER POSSIBILITIES

Type	Advantages / Disadvantages
Natural Fibers	
COTTON	Absorbent, soft, but can be wrinkle prone. Best for glued techniques.
COTTON/SYNTHETIC BLENDS	Slightly less absorbent/softer than cotton, but also less wrinkle-prone.
LINEN	Very crisp, foldable, and elegant, but pressing is essential.
RAYON	Absorbent and soft, but may be too soft to hold a fold. Washability varies. More creaseable when blended with cotton or linen.
PAPER	Absorbent, soft, foldable, and disposable, but size and color range are limited.
Synthetic Fibers	
ACRYLIC	Soft and easy-care, but lacks absorbency and crispness. Also may pill. Best for less-used seasonal napkins or when blended with other natural fibers.
POLYESTER	Washable and wrinkle-resistant, but lacks absorbency, resists folding, and can attract stains.

NOTE: To maximize absorbency, I recommend no more than 50% of the synthetic fiber in the natural/synthetic blend.

FABRIC POSSIBILITIES

❖ *Lightest-weight:* batiste, handkerchief linen, laces, leno.

❖ *Light to medium-weight:* broadcloth, calico prints, chambray, chino, chintz, duck, flannel, gingham, homespun, interlock knits, *Kettlecloth* (and its many imitators), light- to mid-weight linen and denim, muslin, percale, piqué, poplin, sateen, seersucker. Also, sheets.

❖ *Heavier-weight:* damask, double-sided fabrics, homespun, linen, sailcloth, terrycloth.

FABRIC SOURCES: EXHAUST THE POSSIBILITIES

❖ *Your fabric stash.*

❖ *Thrift-shop finds.* Cut out the best sections of vintage curtains, tablecloths, slipcovers, or even a big, full-skirted dress.

❖ *Rummage and garage sales.* Inevitably, crazy prints and colors crop up, for attractive prices like $.25/yard.

❖ *Flat sheets.* Take advantage of white sales and the plentiful napkin yields (see page 93). Indulging in a second flat sheet is a good idea; make it into a coordinating tablecloth.

❖ *Upholstery shops.* Often you can purchase samples at discounted prices. Make a rainbow napkin set out of the same print in several different colors.

❖ *Ready-made napkins* (either new or recycled). Shoddy edges can be refinished; too-small sizes, enlarged; generally dull appearances, embellished. (See "For Napkins Made and Ready-made: No-Sew Embellishments," pages 54 and 66 and "Doctoring Dull (Or Otherwise Undesirable) Ready-mades," page 79.)

❖ *Fabric stores and departments.* For bargains, dig through remnants and flat folds. Investigate all departments— even bridal and childrenswear areas house practical napkin-making materials.

❖ *Mail-order fabric specialists.* See page 94.

FABRIC CONSIDERATIONS: KEY QUESTIONS

❖ *Is it washable and absorbent?*

❖ *Is it vat-dyed?* This type of dye, used on many home-decorator fabrics, is more fade-resistant (unfortunately, also less absorbent). Look for "vat-dyed" on the label or tag. If in doubt, ask a sales clerk—most at least know who to ask.

❖ *Will stain-repellant finishes (like Scotch-gard®) or a high synthetic fiber content impair absorbency?*

❖ *Is there enough fabric* to make the size and number of napkins necessary? Would the cost per napkin actually be lower if you bought a more expensive, wider-width fabric, because of the increased yield? (Refer to the yardage charts on pages 86-91.)

❖ If you are interested in three-dimensional folds, *is the fabric creaseable enough to hold the shape?* (Real linen and tightly-woven cottons work well.)

❖ *Will the wrong side of a one-sided print limit folding options?*

❖ *Is the fabric weight (light to heavy) and construction (loose to tight) well suited to your edge-finishing technique?* (Recommendations are given for each napkin project in this book.)

CARE-FREE NAPKIN CARE

❖ **Store napkins flat.** Stacking large, heavy books (encyclopedias?) on the set, overnight, can cold-press out most wrinkles (Fig. V-10). Uncreased, they'll be ready for folding. (A friend suggests flattening napkins between a box spring and mattress—at my house, our big beds are too heavy, plus the napkins would undoubtedly be forgotten for months.) It does, however, make sense for those with limited cabinet or cupboard storage, to store napkins in large, shallow boxes under the bed.

❖ **Don't touch-up wrinkle-prone napkins until you use them.** No matter how carefully you store them, quick touch-up pressing seems a necessity.

❖ **Enhance the foldability of cotton and linen napkins** by spraying with sizing—or for more crispness, starch—while pressing.

❖ **Treat stains as soon as possible.** Most stains can be removed by soaking in a *cold water/ detergent* solution, treating with a commercial prewash solution and washing in warm water. Repeat the soaking, treating, and washing process, if necessary. *Until the stain is gone, do not subject it to hot water, heat-drying, or pressing—any one of these will heat-set the stain.* Scrape off candle wax with a dull knife; then sandwich the napkin between paper towels and press—the paper will absorb the melted wax. For more detailed stain-removal information, refer to one of the many books on the subject; a current favorite of mine is *Don Aslett's Stainbuster's Bible,* by Don Aslett (©1990, Penguin Books USA, Inc.).

❖ Take a tip from savvy restaurateurs, and *consider white or off-white cotton or linen napkins.* They can be soaked in a mild chlorine-bleach solution, which will remove just about any stain.

❖ *Remember that all-over prints camouflage stains* (a godsend in my household full of active kids and messy adults).

❖ *You can spray napkins with stain-repellant,* such as *Scotch-Gard®,* but I don't recommend it. Napkins are meant to absorb food and beverage stains so your clothes and furniture won't. Also, the chemical smell of the spray can be irritating to sensitive noses. Instead, make a few extra napkins to replace those lost to unsightly stains.

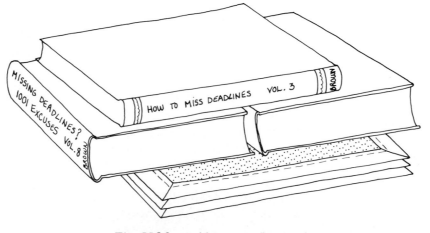

Fig. V-10. *Cold press napkins with large, heavy books.*

DOCTORING DULL (OR OTHERWISE UNDESIRABLE) READY-MADES

❖ **Embellish with fabric paints, fused-and-painted-on appliqués, stenciling, stamping, or glued-on trims** (Fig. V-11). See pages 54 and 66.

❖ **Fuse-and-sew appliqués, quick.** Follow the how-to's on page 54, substituting medium-width, satin-length zigzagging for painting around the edges. See Fig. V-12.

❖ **Add twin-needle or wing-needle topstitching** (Fig. V-13). (See "Handy Notions," page 81).

❖ **Enlarge puny ready-mades** by lapping and edgestitching or serge-seaming four together (Fig. V-14), or by adding edge trim see "18. Lapped-Trim Finish," (page 65).

❖ **Decoratively machine stitch** (Fig. V-15).

❖ **Refinish fraying and/or ugly edges** (Fig. V-16), using any one of the techniques featured in this book.

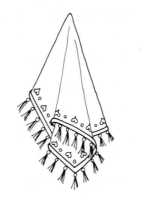

Fig. V-11. *No-sew embellishments!*

Fig. V-12. *Secure appliqués with satin stitching.*

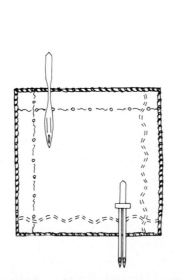

Fig. V-13. *Add twin- or wing-needle topstitching.*

Fig V-14. *Enlarge puny ready-mades.*

Fig. V-15. *Decoratively machine stitch.*

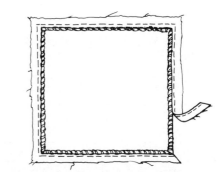

Fig. V-16. *Refinish fraying or ugly edges.*

INSTANT

❖ *Purchased napkin rings* (see pages 28).

❖ *Children's bracelets.*

❖ *Miniature grapevine wreaths* (see page 24). (Stock up during the holidays.)

❖ *Large buckles and T-shirt ties.*

Fig. V-17. *Cover a toilet-paper or paper-towel roll with fabric.*

Fig. V-18. *Cut a 2" (5cm) cross-section.*

Fig. V-19. *Glue on fabric.*

SEMI-INSTANT

❖ *Fabric ribbons and trims* (see pages 46).

❖ *Gift-wrap ribbons.*

❖ *Decorative tasseled cords* (see front cover and page 58).

❖ *Braided or chainstitched cording* (see page 48).

❖ *Fabric-covered toilet-paper or paper-towel roll* (Fig. V-17). With sharp utility scissors, cut a cross-section about 2" (5cm) wide (Fig. V-18). Glue on a 5" (12.5cm) by 6" (15cm) strip of fabric (Fig. V-19). Also see page 20.

❖ *Fabric-crafted napkin rings* (Fig. V-20). For each ring, cut out two strips of matching or coordinating fabric and one strip of fusible transfer web (see page 19), all cut about 2" (5cm) wide by 6" (15cm) long.

1. Sandwich the fusible web between the wrong sides of the two fabric strips; fuse the strips together (Fig. V-21).

2. Finish three raw edges—two long and one short—with narrow rolled or unrolled serged edging (see page 60) or satin stitching (see page 43). See Fig. V-22.

3. Glue the finished short end over the unfinished end, lapping about 1" (2.5cm). See Fig. V-23. Allow to completely dry.

Fig. V-20. *Fabric-craft a napkin ring.*

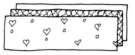

Fig. V-21. *Sandwich fusible web between wrong sides of fabric strips.*

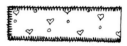

Fig. V-22. *Finish three edges with satin stitching or serging.*

Fig. V-23. *Lap and glue to form napkin ring.*

❖ *Marking pens and/or wheels:* for temporary marking. See Fig. V-24.

❖ *Pinking or scalloping shears:* for finishing edges or hems. See page 21.

❖ *Rotary cutter, large cutting mat, and "T" or "L" rulers:* for the fastest, most accurate cutting (see page 74).

❖ *Permanent washable glue:* for no-sew hemming and tacking. Refer to the "Goof-Proof Gluing Primer," page 18. For glued applications, see pages 29 and 54.

❖ *Twin needles:* for twin-needle topstitched hemming and decorative stitching (Fig. V-25). (Also known as a double needle.) The first number in the size designation is the width between the needles, ranging from 1.6mm to 4.0mm. The wider the space between the needles, the wider the tuck. The second number in the size designation is the needle size, from 11/75 (smallest) to 16/100 (largest). The finer and more lightweight your fabric fibers, the finer the needle should be. For techniques that utilize twin needles, see pages 37 and 53.

❖ *Fusible transfer web:* for making any fabric fusible. Refer to the fusible transfer web section of "No-hassle, No-Sew Tips," page 19. For techniques that utilize fusible transfer web, see pages 25, 29, 45, 54, and 79.

❖ *Ask for these notions at fabric stores or sewing-machine dealerships. If you are unable to find them locally, contact the "Mail-Order Sources," page 94.*

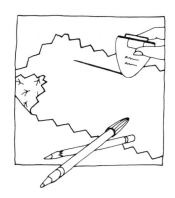

Fig. V-24. *Use washable, water-soluble, or vanishing pens, pencils, or wheels.*

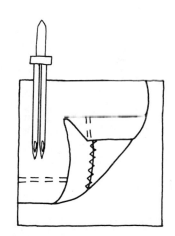

Fig. V-25. *Twin needle—for hemming and decorative topstitching.*

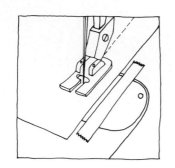

Fig. V-26. *Masking tape as a stitching guide.*

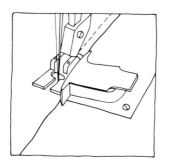

Fig. V-27. *Magnetic stitching guide.*

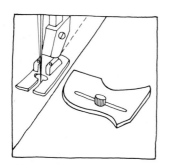

Fig. V-28. *Screw-on stitching guide.*

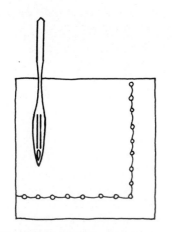

Fig. V-29. *Wing needles for decorative stitching.*

❖ *Transparent tape:* for pin-free basting. For easier removal, use *Scotch™ Brand Magic™ Tape* or one of the other cloudy-tape clones. (You don't have to use tape specified as removable from paper; any transparent-type tape removes easily from fabric.)

❖ *Stitching guides:* for more accurate topstitching, hemming, and decorative stitching. If the distance from the needle to the fabric edge obscures your machine's seam guides, place masking tape on the throat plate (Fig. V-26), or use a magnetic (Fig. V-27) or screw-on guide (Fig. V-28).

❖ *Tear-away nonwovens:* for preventing tunneling and for jam-proofing when starting to stitch at a corner (see page 32). Brands now on the market include Armo® *Tear-Away™*, J & R's *Appliqué-Away™*, and Pellon® *Stitch-n-Tear®*.

❖ *Wing needles:* for decorative stitching. The "wings" on the needle push apart the fabric fibers, creating holes that simulate entredeux trim. See Fig. V-29. The most dramatic results are achieved when stitching through a single layer of crisp, loosely woven fabric. Also available: twin-wing needles, with one (left) winged and one standard needle (Fig. V-30).

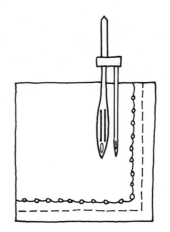

Fig. V-30. *Twin-wing needle decorative stitching.*

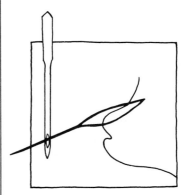

Fig. V-31. *Needle threaders for threading limp or untwisted thread.*

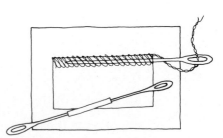

Fig. V-32. *Bury thread tails with tapestry or double-eyed needle.*

- ❖ **Woolly stretch nylon thread:** for better coverage and rolling of narrow rolled serged edges (see page 61). There are several brands to select from: *Woolly Nylon* from YLI, *Bulky Lock* from Coats & Clark, *Metroflock* from Swiss-Metrosene, Corticelli's *S-T-R-E-T-C-H-Y Nylon Thread,* and *Designer's Edge* from Talon. Needle threaders (or dental-bridge floss threader) make threading the untwisted, limp fibers through needle and looper eyes much easier (Fig. V-31).

- ❖ **Fine monofilament nylon thread:** for invisible stitching, and for enhanced rolling of narrow rolled serged edges (see page 61).

- ❖ **Melt-adhesive thread:** for making stitching fusible. Generally the thread is used in the bobbin of a sewing machine or the lower looper of a serger. Two melt-adhesive threads currently available are *ThreadFuse*™ (from The Perfect Notion) and *Stitch 'n Fuse* (from Coats).

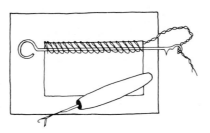

Fig. V-33. *Loop turner and knit-picker also work well for burying threads.*

Fig. V-34. *Coned-thread stand for holding additional cones or spools.*

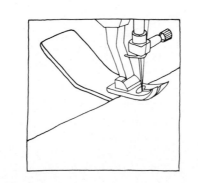

Fig. V-35. *Eliminate jamming with a "shim."*

- ❖ **Seam sealant:** for ravel-proofing thread ends on raw, serged, or sewn edges. Currently *Fray Check*™ by Dritz is the only seam sealant sold to the home-sewing market, although others undoubtedly will be introduced or rereleased.

- ❖ **Large-eyed needles:** for burying heavier decorative thread under the serged stitch. Use a tapestry or double-eyed needle (Fig.V-32). Or substitute a loop turner or knit picker (Fig.V-33).

- ❖ **Coned-thread stand:** for holding additional cones (or spools) of thread when, for better edge coverage, two threads are used in the upper and/or lower loopers (Fig. V-34).

- ❖ **Specialty "shims":** for eliminating jamming at the beginning of a hemmed corner (Fig V-35). Two brands are are the *Hump Jumper* and the *Jean-a-ma-jig*™.

❖ *Special sewing feet:* for ensuring smooth feeding while minimizing stretching and tunneling, such as a satin-edge (Fig. V-36), walking or even-feed (Fig. V-37), or roller foot (Fig. V-38); for preventing running off of cording or braid, such as a special cording (Fig. V-39), embroidery (Fig. V-40), or invisible zipper foot (Fig. V-41); for facilitating even topstitching and pivoting (Fig. V-42). Also, ribbon-application and cording feet are optional attachments for most serger brands and models; ask your dealer.

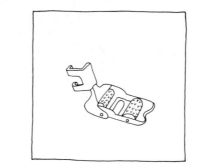

Fig. **V-38**. *Roller foot.*

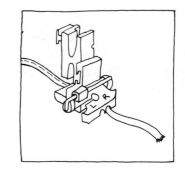

Fig. **V-41**. *Invisible-zipper foot used for cording application.*

Fig. **V-36**. *Satin-edge foot.*

Fig. **V-39**. *Special cording-application foot.*

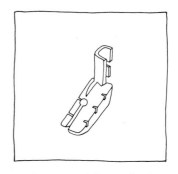

Fig. **V-42**. *Special foot to facilitate even topstitching.*

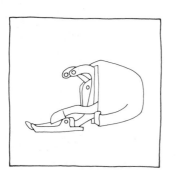

Fig. **V-37**. *Walking or even-feed foot.*

Fig. **V-40**. *Special embroidery foot.*

YARDAGE/YIELD INSIGHTS

Calculating over a thousand yardages (and converting them all into metric equivalents) tends to enlighten one about the sizes, quantities, and fabric widths that provide the best napkin yield. Rather than recommend a similarly intensive calculation session, I've highlighted the parameters followed and insights gleaned while assembling the charts (in hopes that your learning curve will be much shorter).

❖ *The napkin size specified is unfinished or unhemmed.* To determine the finished size, subtract the hems from the size given. For instance, if the size is 18" (46cm), then subtract two times the hem allowance (1/2" or 1.3cm) to arrive at the finished size of 17" (43cm). Uncertain about what size to make? If the yardage and budget allow, always opt for the larger size; larger napkins offer more folding variations and stain protection, and take only seconds more to construct than smaller sizes.

❖ *Sizes charted are the measurement of one side of the napkin square.* Round napkins with the same diameter as the size shown require the same yardage.

❖ So that you won't be short an inch or two, *yardages were rounded up to the next largest standard yardage fraction*, if the yardage calculations fell between standard yardage fractions.

❖ *Both imperial (inches/yards) and metric (meters/centimeters) charts are included* for the convenience of my readers worldwide.

❖ *Note the +Maximum-napkin-yield tip given at the bottom of each fabric width chart.* These tips provide helpful hints on which size napkins, in what quantities, yield the most napkins and the least waste for that size.

❖ *Be forewarned that actual fabric width often varies from what is specified on the bolt end or label.* Play it smart: *measure the fabric width first.* Find the closest fabric-width chart (see pages 86 – 91), or custom calculate: divide the actual yardage by 2, 3, 4, 5 (or more if it's super-wide) and when the division results in a napkin size you like, that's the one to use (even if it includes a fraction). You won't waste any fabric width, although there may be some leftover length.

❖ *All yields shown on the charts are rounded up to the nearest eighth of a yard or tenth of a meter.* Because I've rounded up, you may occasionally be able to yield the same number of napkins when using slightly less or narrower fabric.

❖ For 120" (305cm)-wide fabric, simply *double the yardage* requirements for 60" (150cm)-wide fabric.

NAPKIN YARDAGE YIELDS FOR 36"-WIDE FABRIC

Size	Number of Napkins								
	4	6	8	10	12	14	16	18	20
12"	2/3	2/3	1	1-1/3	1-1/3	1-2/3	2	2	2-1/3
15"	7/8	1-1/4	1-3/4	2-1/8	2-1/2	3	3-1/3	3-3/4	4-1/4
18"	1	1-1/2	2	2-1/2	3	3-1/2	4	4-1/2	5
20"	2-1/4	3-1/3	4-1/2	5-5/8	6-3/4	7-7/8	9	10	11-1/8
24"	2-2/3	4	5-1/3	6-2/3	8	9-1/3	10-2/3	12	13-1/3
26"	3	4-1/3	5-7/8	7-1/4	8-3/4	10-1/8	11-5/8	13	14-1/2

The napkin sizes specified are unfinished or unhemmed. To determine the finished size, subtract the hems from the size given.

Maximum-napkin-yield tip: Cut 12" (six per 2/3 yard) or 18" (four per 1 yard) squares. Napkin multiples of three (for the 12" size) or two (for the 18" size) will waste little or no fabric (see the shaded yardages, above). For instance, twelve of the 12"-size napkins (1-1/3 yards required) or six of the 18"-size napkins (1-1/2 yards required) will utilize the entire piece (or nearly so) of 36"-wide fabric.

NAPKIN METRIC YIELDS FOR 90CM-WIDE FABRIC

Size	Number of Napkins								
	4	6	8	10	12	14	16	18	20
30cm	.6	.6	.9	1.2	1.2	1.5	1.8	1.8	2.1
38cm	.8	1.1	1.6	1.9	2.3	2.7	3	3.4	3.9
46cm	.9	1.4	1.8	2.3	2.7	3.2	3.7	4.1	4.6
51cm	2	3	4.1	5.1	6.1	7.2	8.2	9.1	10.2
61cm	2.4	3.7	4.9	6	7.3	8.5	9.7	11	12.2
66cm	2.7	4	5.4	6.6	8	9.3	10.6	11.9	13.3

The napkin sizes specified are unfinished or unhemmed. To determine the finished size, subtract the hems from the size given.

Maximum-napkin-yield tip: Cut 30cm (six per .6 meter) or 46cm (four per .9 meter) squares. Napkin multiples of three (for the 30cm size) or two (for the 46cm size) will waste little or no fabric (see the shaded areas, above). For instance, twelve of the 30cm-size napkins (1.2 meters required) or six of the 46cm-size napkins (1.4 meters required) will utilize the entire piece (or nearly so) of 90cm-wide fabric.

Napkin Yardage Yields for 45"-Wide Fabric

Size	Number of Napkins								
	4	**6**	**8**	**10**	**12**	**14**	**16**	**18**	**20**
12"	2/3	2/3	1	1-1/3	1-1/3	1-2/3	2	2	2-1/3
15"	7/8	7/8	1-1/4	1-2/3	1-2/3	2-1/8	2-1/2	2-1/2	3
18"	1	1-1/2	2	2-1/2	3	3-1/2	4	4-1/2	5
20"	1-1/8	1-2/3	2-1/4	2-7/8	3-1/3	4	4-1/2	5	5-5/8
22-1/2"	1-1/4	1-7/8	2-1/2	3-1/8	3-3/4	4-3/8	5	5-5/8	6-1/4
24"	2-2/3	4	5-1/3	6-2/3	8	9-1/3	10-2/3	12	13-1/3

The napkin sizes specified are unfinished or unhemmed. To determine the finished size, subtract the hems from the size given.

Maximum-napkin-yield tip: Cut 15" (six per 2/3 yard) or 22-1/2" (four per 1-1/4 yards) squares. Napkin multiples of three (for the 15" size) or two (for the 22-1/2" size) will waste little or no fabric (see the shaded yardages, above). For instance, twelve of the 15"-size napkins (1-2/3 yards required) or eight of the 22-1/2"-size napkins (2-1/2 yards required) will utilize the entire piece (or nearly so) of 45"-wide fabric.

Napkin Metric Yields for 115cm-Wide Fabric

Size	Number of Napkins								
	4	**6**	**8**	**10**	**12**	**14**	**16**	**18**	**20**
30cm	.6	.6	.9	1.2	1.2	1.5	1.8	1.8	2.1
38cm	.8	.8	1.1	1.5	1.5	1.9	2.3	2.3	2.7
46cm	.9	1.4	1.8	2.3	2.7	3.2	3.7	4.1	4.6
51cm	1	1.5	2	2.6	3	3.7	4.1	4.6	5.2
57cm	1.1	1.7	2.3	2.9	3.4	4	4.6	5.2	5.7
61cm	2.4	3.7	4.9	6	7.3	8.5	9.7	11	12.2

The napkin sizes specified are unfinished or unhemmed. To determine the finished size, subtract the hems from the size given.

Maximum-napkin-yield tip: Cut 38cm (six per .8 meter) or 57cm (four per 1.1 meters) squares. Napkin multiples of three (for the 38cm size) or two (for the 57cm size) will waste little or no fabric (see the shaded areas, above). For instance, twelve of the 38cm-size napkins (1.5 meters required) or eight of the 57cm-size napkins (2.3 meters required) will utilize the entire piece (or nearly so) of 115cm fabric.

NAPKIN YARDAGE YIELDS FOR 54/55"-WIDE FABRIC

Size	Number of Napkins								
	4	6	8	10	12	14	16	18	20
12"	1/3	2/3	2/3	1	1	1-1/3	1-1/3	1-2/3	1-2/3
15"	7/8	7/8	1-1/4	1-2/3	1-2/3	2-1/8	2-1/2	2-1/2	3
18"	1	1	1-1/2	2	2	2-1/2	3	3	3-1/2
20"	1-1/8	1-2/3	2-1/4	2-7/8	3-1/3	4	4-1/2	5	5-5/8
24"	1-1/3	2	2-2/3	3-1/3	4	4-2/3	5-1/3	6	6-2/3
27"	1-1/2	2-1/4	3	3-3/4	4-1/2	5-1/4	6	6-3/4	7-1/2

The napkin sizes specified are unfinished or unhemmed. To determine the finished size, subtract the hems from the size given.

Maximum-napkin-yield Tip: Cut 18" (six per 1 yard) or 27" (four per 1-1/2 yards) squares. Napkin multiples of three (for the 18" size) or two (for the 27" size) will waste little or no fabric (see the shaded yardages, above). For instance, six of the 18"-size napkins (1 yard required) or six of the 27"-size napkins (2-1/4 yards required) will utilize the entire piece (or nearly so) of 54/55"-wide fabric.

NAPKIN METRIC YIELDS FOR 140CM-WIDE FABRIC

Size	Number of Napkins								
	4	6	8	10	12	14	16	18	20
30cm	.3	.6	.6	.9	.9	1.2	1.2	1.5	1.5
38cm	.8	.8	1.1	1.5	1.5	1.9	2.3	2.3	2.7
46cm	.9	.9	1.4	1.8	1.8	2.3	2.7	2.7	3.2
51cm	1	1.5	2	2.6	3	3.7	4.1	4.6	5.1
61cm	1.2	1.8	2.4	3	3.7	4.3	4.9	5.5	6
69cm	1.4	2	2.7	3.4	4.1	4.8	5.5	6.1	6.9

The napkin sizes specified are unfinished or unhemmed. To determine the finished size, subtract the hems from the size given.

Maximum-napkin-yield Tip: Cut 46cm (six per .9 meter) or 69cm (four per 1.4 meters) squares. Napkin multiples of three (for the 46cm size) or two (for the 69cm size) will waste little or no fabric (see the shaded areas, above). For instance, six of the 46cm-size napkins (.9 meter required) or six of the 69cm-size napkins (2 meters required) will utilize the entire piece (or nearly so) of 140cm-wide fabric.

Napkin Yardage Yields for 60"-Wide Fabric

Size	Number of Napkins								
	4	6	8	10	12	14	16	18	20
12"	1/3	2/3	2/3	2/3	1	1	1-1/3	1-1/3	1-1/3
15"	1/2	7/8	7/8	1-1/4	1-1/4	1-2/3	1-2/3	2-1/8	2-1/8
18"	1	1	1-1/2	2	2	2-1/2	3	3	3-1/2
20"	1-1/8	1-1/8	1-2/3	2-1/4	2-1/4	2-7/8	3-1/3	3-1/3	4
24"	1-1/3	1-1/3	2	3-1/3	4	4-2/3	5-1/3	6	6-2/3
26"	1-1/2	2-1/4	3	3-5/8	4-1/3	5-1/8	5-7/8	6-1/2	7-1/4

The napkin sizes specified are unfinished or unhemmed. To determine the finished size, subtract the hems from the size given.

Maximum-napkin-yield Tip: Cut 12" (ten per 2/3 yard), 15" (twelve per 1-1/4 yards), or 20" (twelve per 2-1/4 yards) squares. Napkin multiples of five (for the 12" size), four (for the 15" size), or three (for the 20" size) will waste little or no fabric (see the shaded yardages, above). For instance, twenty of the 12"-size napkins (1-1/3 yards required), eight of the 15"-size napkins (7/8 yards required), or six of the 20"-size napkins (1-1/8 yards required) will utilize the entire piece (or nearly so) of 60"-wide fabric.

Napkin Metric Yields for 150cm-Wide Fabric

Size	Number of Napkins								
	4	6	8	10	12	14	16	18	20
30cm	.3	.6	.6	.6	.9	.9	1.2	1.2	1.2
38cm	.5	.8	.8	1.1	1.1	1.5	1.5	1.9	1.9
46cm	.9	.9	1.4	1.8	1.8	2.3	2.7	2.7	3.2
51cm	1	1	1.5	2	2	2.6	3	3	3.7
61cm	1.2	1.2	1.8	3	3.7	4.3	4.9	5.5	6
66cm	1.4	2	2.7	3.3	4	4.7	5.4	5.9	6.6

The napkin sizes specified are unfinished or unhemmed. To determine the finished size, subtract the hems from the size given.

Maximum-napkin-yield Tip: Cut 30cm (ten per .6 meter), 38cm (twelve per 1.1 meters), or 51cm (twelve per 2 meters) squares. Napkin multiples of five (for the 30cm size), four (for the 38cm size), or three (for the 51cm size) will waste little or no fabric (see the shaded areas, above). For instance, twenty of the 30cm-size napkins (1.2 meters required), eight of the 38cm-size napkins (.8 meter required), or six of the 51cm-size napkins (1 meter required) will utilize the entire piece (or nearly so) of 150cm-wide fabric.

Napkin Yardage Yields for 72"-Wide Fabric

Size	Number of Napkins								
	4	**6**	**8**	**10**	**12**	**14**	**16**	**18**	**20**
12"	1/3	1/3	2/3	2/3	2/3	1	1	1	1-1/3
15"	1/2	7/8	7/8	1-1/4	1-1/4	1-2/3	1-2/3	2-1/8	2-1/8
18"	1/2	1	1	1-1/2	1-1/2	2	2	2-1/2	2-1/2
20"	1-1/8	1-1/8	1-2/3	2-1/4	2-1/4	2-7/8	3-1/3	3-1/3	4
24"	1-1/3	1-1/3	2	2-2/3	2-2/3	3-1/3	4	4	4-2/3
26"	1-1/2	2-1/4	3	3-5/8	4-1/3	5-1/8	5-7/8	6-1/2	7-1/4

The napkin sizes specified are unfinished or unhemmed. To determine the finished size, subtract the hems from the size given.

Maximum-napkin-yield Tip: Cut 12" (eighteen per 1 yard), 18" (eight per 1 yard) or 24" (six per 1-1/3 yards) squares. Napkin multiples of six (for the 12" size), four (for the 18" size), or three (for the 24" size) will waste little or no fabric (see the shaded yardages, above). For instance, six of the 12"-size napkins (1/3 yard required), eight of the 18"-size napkins (1 yard required), or six of the 24"-size napkins (1-1/3 yards required) will utilize the entire piece (or nearly so) of 72"-wide fabric.

Napkin Metric Yields for 180cm-Wide Fabric

Size	Number of Napkins								
	4	**6**	**8**	**10**	**12**	**14**	**16**	**18**	**20**
30cm	.3	.3	.6	.6	.6	.9	.9	.9	1.2
38cm	.5	.8	.8	1.1	1.1	1.5	1.5	1.9	1.9
46cm	.5	.9	.9	1.4	1.4	1.8	1.8	2.3	2.3
51cm	1	1	1.5	2	2	2.6	3	3	3.7
61cm	1.2	1.2	1.8	2.4	2.4	3	3.7	3.7	4.3
66cm	1.4	2	2.7	3.3	4	4.7	5.4	5.9	6.6

The napkin sizes specified are unfinished or unhemmed. To determine the finished size, subtract the hems from the size given.

Maximum-napkin-yield Tip: Cut 30cm (eighteen per .9 meter), 46cm (eight per .9 meter) or 61cm (six per 1.2 meters) squares. Napkin multiples of six (for the 30cm size), four (for the 46cm size), or three (for the 61cm size) will waste little or no fabric (see the shaded areas, above). For instance, six of the 30cm-size napkins (.3 meter required), eight of the 46cm-size napkins (.9 meter required), or six of the 61cm-size napkins (1.2 meters required) will utilize the entire piece (or nearly so) of 180cm-wide fabric.

Napkin Yardage Yields for 90"-Wide Fabric

Size	Number of Napkins								
	4	6	8	10	12	14	16	18	20
12"	1/3	1/3	2/3	2/3	2/3	2/3	1	1	1
15"	1/2	1/2	7/8	7/8	7/8	1-1/4	1-1/4	1-1/4	1-2/3
18"	1/2	1	1	1	1-1/2	1-1/2	2	2	2
20"	5/8	1-1/8	1-1/8	1-2/3	1-2/3	2-1/4	2-1/4	2-7/8	2-7/8
22-1/2"	5/8	1-1/4	1-1/4	1-7/8	1-7/8	2-1/2	2-1/2	3-1/8	3-1/8
24"	1-1/3	1-1/3	2	2-2/3	2-2/3	3-1/3	4	4	4-2/3
30"	1-2/3	1-2/3	2-1/2	3-1/3	3-1/3	4-1/4	5	5	5-7/8

The napkin sizes specified are unfinished or unhemmed. To determine the finished size, subtract the hems from the size given.

Maximum-napkin-yield Tip: Cut 15" (six per 1/2 yard), 18" (ten per 1 yard), 22-1/2" (four per 5/8 yard), or 30" (six per 1-2/3 yard) squares. Napkin multiples of six (for the 15" size), five (for the 18" size), four (for the 22-1/2" size), or three (for the extra-large 30" size) will waste little or no fabric (see the shaded yardages, above). For instance, twelve of the 15"-size napkins (7/8 yard required), twenty of the 18" size napkin(1 yard required), eight of the 22-1/2"-size napkins (1-1/4 yards required), or twelve of the 30"-size napkins (3-1/3

Napkin Metric Yields for 230cm-Wide Fabric

Size	Number of Napkins								
	4	6	8	10	12	14	16	18	20
30cm	.3	.3	.6	.6	.6	.6	.9	.9	.9
38cm	.5	.5	.8	.8	.8	1.1	1.1	1.1	1.5
46cm	.5	.9	.9	.9	1.4	1.4	1.8	1.8	1.8
51cm	.6	1	1	1.5	1.5	2	2	2.6	2.6
57cm	.6	1.1	1.1	1.7	1.7	2.3	2.3	2.9	2.9
61cm	1.2	1.2	1.8	2.4	2.4	3	3.7	3.7	4.3
73cm	1.5	1.5	2.3	3	3	3.9	4.6	4.6	5.4

The napkin sizes specified are unfinished or unhemmed. To determine the finished size, subtract the hems from the size given.

Maximum-napkin-yield Tip: Cut 38cm (six per .5 meter), 46cm (ten per .9 meter), or 57cm (four per .6 meter), or 73cm (six per 1.5 meters) squares. Napkin multiples of six (for the 38cm size), five (for the 46cm size), or three (for the extra-large 73cm size) will waste little or no fabric (see the shaded areas, above). For instance, twelve of the 38cm-size napkins (.8 meter required), ten of the 46cm- size napkins (.9 meter required), eight of the 57cm-size napkins (1.1 meters required), or twelve of the 73cm-size napkins (3 meters required) will utilize the entire piece (or nearly so) of 230cm-wide fabric.

Napkin Yields for Border Prints

THE GOOD NEWS: border prints make beautiful napkins and add design intrigue to any folding scheme. THE BAD NEWS: cut and seamed in a chevroned motif, the yardage requirements can be budget-breaking (best to find these on flat-fold bargain tables). But the ample leftover yardage can be fully utilized for coordinating napkin linings, napkin rings (see page 80), tablecloths, and runners.

As a design alternative to the more yardage-costly layouts featured below, cut a runner or runners out of the border print, and napkins out of the leftover, borderless section. See Fig. V-43.

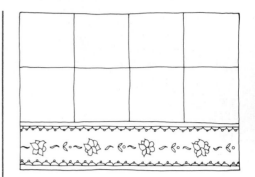

Fig. V-43. *Design alternative: cut runner out of border, napkins out of all-over print or solid.*

CORNER-ACCENT BORDER DESIGN

Any border-print fabric, 20" (51 cm)-wide or wider. See Fig. V-44.

15" (38CM) SIZE:

FOUR NAPKINS:	2-1/4 yards (2 meters)
SIX NAPKINS:	3-1/3 yards (3 meters)
EIGHT NAPKINS:	4-1/2 yards (4.1 meters)

18" (46CM) SIZE:

FOUR NAPKINS:	2-2/3 yards (2.4 meters)
SIX NAPKINS:	4 yards (3.7 meters)
EIGHT NAPKINS:	5-1/3 yards (4.8 meters)

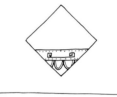

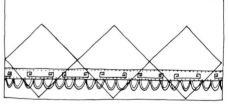

Fig. V-44. *Corner-accent border design.*

SINGLE-SIDED BORDER DESIGN

Any border-print fabric, 20" (51 cm)-wide or wider. See Fig. V-45.

15" (38CM) SIZE:

FOUR NAPKINS:	1-3/4 yards 1.6 meters)
SIX NAPKINS:	2-1/2 yards (2.3 meters)
EIGHT NAPKINS:	3-1/3 yards (3 meters)

18" (46CM) SIZE:

FOUR NAPKINS:	2 yards (1.8 meters)
SIX NAPKINS:	3 yards (2.7 meters)
EIGHT NAPKINS:	4 yards (3.7 meters)
TEN NAPKINS:	5 yards (4.6 meters)

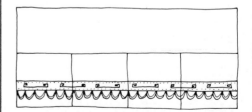

Fig. V-45. *Single-sided border design.*

Napkin Yields for Flat Sheets

All sheet sizes vary brand to brand, although those specified below are reasonably standard.

To yield more napkins per sheet, pull and press out the top and bottom hems.

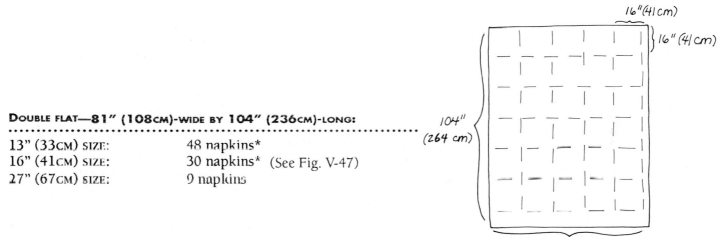

Fig. V-46. Twin flat sheet.

Twin flat—66" (168cm)-wide by 104" (236cm)-long:

12" (31cm) size:	40 napkins*
16-1/2" (42cm) size:	24 napkins* (See Fig. V-46)
22" (56cm) size:	12 napkins

Double flat—81" (108cm)-wide by 104" (236cm)-long:

13" (33cm) size:	48 napkins*
16" (41cm) size:	30 napkins* (See Fig. V-47)
27" (67cm) size:	9 napkins

Fig. V-47. Double flat sheet.

Queen flat—90" (117cm)-wide by 110" (247cm)-long:

12" (31cm) size:	63 napkins*
15" (38cm) size:	42 napkins*
18" (46cm) size:	30 napkins* (See Fig. V-48)
22-1/2" (57cm) size:	12 napkins

*Best sizes to maximize yield

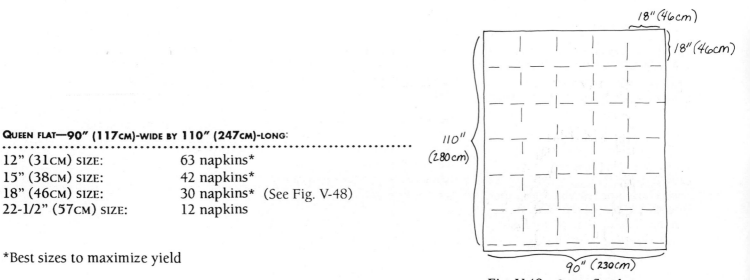

Fig. V-48. Queen flat sheet.

MAIL-ORDER SOURCES

First, please visit your local fabric retailer. However, for those who live in remote areas, or who simply can't shop, I've included this list. Unfortunately, in this small space, I cannot possibly cover all the mail-order sources. (Believe me, there are many more.) It supplements the extensive mail-order list in my book, *Innovative Sewing* (available for $16.95 postpaid—$18.10 for California residents from Open Chain—see below). Also, consult *Designer Source Listing,* Volume IV, by Maryanne Burgess, © 1989 ($19.95 postpaid from Carikean Publishing, P.O. Box 11771, Chicago, Il 60611-0771), and the mail-order ads in national sewing publications.

Attention: If you're reading this more than a year after publication, send a stamped, self-addressed envelope to Open Chain Publishing, Inc., P.O. Box 2634-B, Menlo Park, CA 94026, for a free update.

AARDVARK ADVENTURES
P.O. Box 2449
Livermore, CA 94551
(800/388-2687)
Rayon and other decorative threads, assorted notions, and lots of fun. Catalog/newspaper, $1.

CALICO CORNERS
Call 1-800/821-7700, ext. 810, for the retail outlet nearest you. Complete home-decorating supplies, from fabrics to findings.

CLOTILDE, INC.
1909 SW First Ave.
Ft. Lauderdale, FL 33315
(305/761-8655)
Special machine feet and accessories, threads, fusible transfer web, glues, and much more. Send $1 for first-class delivery of color catalog.

THE FABRIC CENTER
488 Electric Ave. P.O. Box 8212
Fitchburg, MA 01420-8212
(508/343-4402)
Offers discounts on most major decorator fabrics. Free brochure.

FABRIC EDITIONS, LTD.
Honey Hill Farm
89A Hayden Rowe
Hopkinton, MA 01748
(800/242-5684 or 508/435-9645)
Calico prints, affordably priced. $11 for the complete set of six color cards and a year of swatched mailings.

FABRICLAND, INC.
Box 20235
Portland, OR 97220
(800/255-5412)
Quantity discounts on a wide range of fabrics and notions. Minimum order, $50. Write for their price list.

G STREET FABRICS
11854 Rockville Pike
Rockville, MD 20852
(301/231-8960)
Extensive decorator offerings. Custom samples, $5 (for up to 10, refundable). Notion product listings, $4.

HANCOCK FABRICS
3841 Hinkleville Rd.
Paducah, KY 42001
(800/626-2723, orders only)
Send a pre-addressed stamped, large envelope for product and fabric listings.

HOMESPUN WEAVERS
55 South Seventh Street
Emmaus, PA 18049
(215/967-455).
Lovely homespun fabrics. Color brochure and swatches, $2.

KEEPSAKE QUILTING
Dover Street, P.O. Box 1459,
Meredith, NH 03253.
(603/279-3351)
Hundreds of 100% cotton calico prints. Free catalog.

NANCY'S NOTIONS, LTD.
P.O. Box 683
Beaver Dam, WI
(800/765-0690)
Wide-width decorator fabrics, plus decorative threads, glues, fusible transfer web, and machine accessories. Free color catalog.

THE PERFECT NOTION
566 Hoyt Street
Darien, CT 06820
(203/968-1257)
Hard-to-find notions and threads, including their *Thread Fuse™*. Catalog, $1.

SERGE & SEW NOTIONS AND FABRICS
11285 96th Ave. N.
Maple Grove, MN 56369
(800/969-7396)
Decorative threads, serger and sewing machine parts and feet, plus interesting notions of all kinds. Color catalog, $2.50 (refundable).

SEW/FIT CO.
P.O. Box 565
La Grange, IL 60525
(312/579-3222)
Notions, cutting tools, and mats. Catalog, $3 (refundable).

SPEED STITCH
3113-D Broadpoint Dr.
Harbor Heights, FL 33983
(800/874-4115)
Rayon threads and other machine-art supplies. Color catalog, $3 (refundable with order).

TREADLEART
25834 Narbonne Ave., Ste. I
Lomita, CA 90717
(800/327-4222)
Notions, decorative threads, and machine accessories. Bimonthly magazine, $12 annually. Catalog, $2.

FABRIC CREDITS

Most of the fabrics photographed in this book were donated by the generous companies who continually support my work and the home-sewing/craft industries. Although only one or two can be ordered directly, I encourage you to ask for these lines at your local fabric store or department. Showing them a picture from the book should help in your search. Because of ever-changing fabric styles, you may not be able to locate the specific fabrics shown, but you should be able to locate a close facsimile or a perfectly suitable substitute.

Wholesale accounts: Write me for company addresses c/o Open Chain Publishing, Inc., PO Box 2634-B, Menlo Park, CA 94026

FRONT COVER: Fabric Traditions.

PAGE 20: 1. *Pink Now, Sew (Maybe) Later*. Folded (napkin and lining): VIP Fabrics. Unfolded (napkin and lining): same as folded napkin (lining side is showing).

PAGE 22: 2. *Fringe Now, Sew Later*. Folded napkin: Homespun Weavers (see "Mail-Order Sources," page 94). Unfolded napkin: Delta Mills. Background: Spartex.

PAGE 24: 3. *Fabric-Fringed Edges*. Folded (napkin and lining): Alexander Henry. Unfolded (napkin and lining): same as folded napkin (lining side is showing).

PAGE 26: 4. *Great Glue! Trimmed Hems*. Folded napkin: Dan River, Inc. Unfolded napkin: Fabric Wholesalers (see Fabricland, Inc., under "Mail-Order Sources," page 94). Offray ribbons.

PAGE 28: 5. *Fast-Fused Edges*. Folded napkin: Fabric Traditions. Unfolded napkin: Fabric Traditions.

PAGE 34: 6. *Lined Napkins—in Minutes!* Folded (napkin and lining): Spartex (some colors available through Nancy's Notions, Ltd.—see "Mail-Order Sources," page 94). Unfolded (napkin and lining): Spartex.

PAGE 36: 7. *Twin-Needle Topstitched Hems*. Folded napkin: Concord Fabrics. Unfolded napkins: damask-look print, Concord Fabrics; pink chintz, Lanscot-Arlen; ivory lace, Americana.

PAGE 38: 8. *Hemmed and Satin-Stitched Edges*. Folded and unfolded napkin: Waverly (by Schumacher).

PAGE 40: 9. *Narrow Hems, Posthaste*. Folded napkin: Fabric Traditions. Unfolded napkin: Lanscot-Arlen.

PAGE 42: 10. *Double Satin-Stitched Edges*. Folded napkin, unfolded napkin, and background: Creative Home Textiles.

PAGE 44: 11. *Decoratively Machine-Stitched Edges*. Folded (napkin and lining) and unfolded (napkin and lining): Fabric Traditions.

PAGE 46: 12. *Easy Trimmed Edges*. Folded and unfolded napkin: VIP Fabrics. Offray ribbon.

PAGE 48: 13. *Hidden-Seam Trim Finish*. Folded (napkin and lining) and unfolded napkin: VIP Fabrics. Background: Americana.

PAGE 50: 14. *No-Measure Miters*. Folded (napkin and lining), unfolded napkin and background: Creative Home Textiles.

PAGE 58: 15. *Simple: Serged, Turned, & Topstitched*. Folded and unfolded napkin: Fabric Traditions. Background: Spartex.

PAGE 60: 16. *Narrow Rolled-Edge Finish*. Folded and unfolded napkins: Concord Fabrics.

PAGE 62: 17. *Unrolled-Edge Finish*. Folded and unfolded napkins: Concord Fabrics. Background: Lanscot-Arlen.

PAGE 64: 18. *Lapped-Trim Finish*. Folded and unfolded napkins: Fabric Traditions. Offray ribbon.

BACK COVER: Fabric Traditions. Offray ribbon.

INDEX

———◆◆———

Additional softbound copies of *Quick Napkin Creations* are available from:

Open Chain Publishing, Inc.
P.O. Box 2634-B
Menlo Park, CA 94026
(415) 366-4440

$15.00 *postpaid* ($16.00, California *residents*)

Wholesale inquiries and bulk orders welcome.

We publish other good sewing books, like *The Busy Woman's Sewing Book* and *The Busy Woman's Fitting Book*, both by Nancy Zieman, and *Claire Shaeffer's Sewing S.O.S.* Please write for a free list and a sample of our quarterly newsletter, "The Creative Machine." Meanwhile, hug your sewing machine.